COMBAT AIRCRAFT

144 B-36 'PEACEMAKER' UNITS
OF THE COLD WAR

SERIES EDITOR TONY HOLMES

144

COMBAT AIRCRAFT

Peter E Davies

B-36 'PEACEMAKER' UNITS OF THE COLD WAR

OSPREY
PUBLISHING

OSPREY PUBLISHING
Bloomsbury Publishing Plc
Kemp House, Chawley Park, Cumnor Hill, Oxford, OX2 9PH, UK
29 Earlsfort Terrace, Dublin 2, Ireland
1385 Broadway, 5th Floor, New York, NY 10018, USA
E-mail; info@ospreypublishing.com
www.ospreypublishing.com

OSPREY is a trademark of Osprey Publishing Ltd

First published in Great Britain in 2022

A catalogue record for this book is available from the British Library.

ISBN; PB 9781472850393; eBook 9781472850409;
ePDF 9781472850416; XML 9781472850423

22 23 24 25 26   10 9 8 7 6 5 4 3 2 1

Edited by Tony Holmes
Cover Artwork by Gareth Hector
Aircraft Profiles by Jim Laurier
Index by Janet Andrew
Typeset by PDQ Digital Media Solutions, UK
Printed and bound in India by Replika Press Private Ltd

Osprey Publishing supports the Woodland Trust, the UK's leading woodland
conservation charity.

To find out more about our authors and books visit **www.ospreypublishing.com**.
Here you will find extracts, author interviews, details of forthcoming events and
the option to sign up for our newsletter.

Front Cover

B-36J-5 52-2225 flew with the 26th BS/
11th BW from Carswell AFB, Texas. It was
one of the aircraft that deployed to
Nouasseur AFB, French Morocco, in May
1956 at around the time of the Suez Crisis,
flying on to Dhahran AB, Saudi Arabia, in a
show of force. The return flight to Carswell
took more than 30 hours. It deployed to
Nouasseur again in the autumn of 1956
during the Lebanon Crisis, the aircraft being
armed with 20 megaton Mk 14/24 nuclear
weapons. SAC bomber deployments to
Nouasseur and Sidi Slimane (also in
Morocco) began in August 1954 with whole
wings of B-47s in Operation *Leap Frog*.
Flown by Capt Patrick O'Malley's crew,
52-2225 was one of two 11th BW B-36Js
that won back the Fairchild Trophy in 1956,
beating several B-47 units in the process.
It was converted to 'Featherweight'
configuration in 1957 and then retired to
the MASDC at Davis-Monthan AFB with
2500 hours on the airframe (*Cover artwork
by Gareth Hector*)

Previous Pages

B-36B-5 44-92038 with a factory-applied
Project GEM Arctic red paint scheme,
chosen because fluorescent Day-Glo
colours were not yet available. Converted to
D-model configuration, the bomber was lost
at Fort Worth in June 1952 when a spark
caused an uncontrollable fire during
refuelling (*Terry Panopalis Collection*)

CONTENTS

CHAPTER ONE

BIGGER AND BOLDER

The largest bomber ever to have served with the US Air Force (USAF) still rates numerous superlatives decades after the last example flew. With an unmatched 86,000-lb bomb load, an unrefuelled range greater than the B-2A Spirit's and a 230-ft wingspan, the Convair B-36 earned its unofficial name 'Peacemaker' by maintaining America's nuclear deterrent throughout a long Cold War period, during which Soviet defences gradually developed the means to resist its power.

On 8 September 1945, the first XB-36 emerged from the massive Fort Worth, Texas, Government Aircraft Plant 4, the home of the Consolidated Vultee Aircraft Corporation as it became in 1943, abbreviated thereafter to Convair from 1954. The proximity of Lake Worth was originally an incentive to use this as a main manufacturing plant, rather than the company's San Diego, California, headquarters, as its newly completed PBY Catalina flying boats could be flown from there. Fear of Japanese attacks on the US west coast also prompted a move into safer territory in Texas.

The huge bomber's development had begun in 1941, but it was delayed by America's entry into World War 2 following the Japanese attack on Pearl Harbor, and the subsequent need to use Plant 4's cavernous interior to build 2743 B-24 Liberator bombers, together with B-32 Dominators, PBY Catalinas and C-87 Liberator Express transport aircraft.

It was the shock of the Pearl Harbor raid on 7 December 1941 that persuaded the US War Department to expedite the development of a

Accompanied by a C-87 transport version of Consolidated's legendary B-24 Liberator bomber, XB-36 prototype 42-13570 makes an early test flight. Both machines are having to fly nose-high in order to remain in formation with the slower photo-aircraft. The 'buzz number' BM-570 was painted on the nose and below the left wing of 42-13570 at a later date (*Terry Panopalis Collection*) bomber with far greater range and payload than the B-17 Flying Fortress or the B-24 Liberator. The aircraft's origins coincided with the building of Plant 4, begun in April 1941 on the understanding that the factory could be suitable for the manufacture of an intercontinental bomber with a range of 10,000 miles, a wingspan of 195 ft and an unprecedented weight of 200,000 lbs – four times that of a loaded B-24.

Although the decision to delay its development was understandable in a wartime situation where mass production of established types like the B-24 and higher-risk innovations like the Boeing B-29 Superfortress was vital, the B-36 might have been ready to attack Japan from Hawaii in 1944 had it been prioritised in 1941.

The idea of a massive intercontinental bomber also emerged as the 'Amerika bomber', conceived in 1940 to fulfil Adolf Hitler's vision of bombing New York and 20 other targets in the USA if America was drawn into World War 2. The four-engined Messerschmitt Me 264 and the six-engined Junkers Ju 390, with a 165-ft wingspan, were intended to make the 7200-mile round trip from Europe via the Azores with light bomb loads. They reached prototype form only.

In Britain, the Bristol Aeroplane Company made preliminary designs in 1937 for a large bomber with wings spanning 230 ft – the same as the B-36, but with a 15-ft longer fuselage. With eight paired 2650 hp Centaurus engines driving contra-rotating 16-ft diameter propellers, the Type 167 would have had a 5500-mile range at 250 mph. By 1948 the design had evolved into the Brabazon 100-seat airliner – a commercial failure which also reached prototype form only, but completed successful flight trials. In April 1949, the Brabazon's designated test pilot, Bill Pegg, visited Convair for familiarisation training on the XB-36.

Six-engined giant bomber designs were also pursued in the Soviet Union from the early 1930s with the ANT-16, its wings spanning 177 ft, and the aircraft's even larger eight-engined derivative, the ANT-20 *Maxim Gorky*. It boasted a 206 ft 8 in wingspan. Japan's six-engined G10N1 had the same wingspan, and it was designed to reach America.

The XB-36's nose, seen here in June 1947, included a smaller 'greenhouse' area with its bomb-aiming window placed centrally. Crew access was via a ladder in the nose-gear well (*Terry Panopalis Collection*)

A much earlier project to build a six-engined, long-range bomber (and the only six-engined American aircraft constructed and flown prior to the B-36) actually originated in the USA as a response to the Zeppelin-Staaken R.VI biplanes that had operated over the Western Front from 1917. Walter Barling's 1923 XNBL-1 triplane experimental night bomber, built by Wittemann-Lewis, had a wing span of 120 ft. Its six 400 hp Liberty engines gave it a cruising speed of only 60 mph and a service ceiling of a mere 7700 ft. Carrying bombs reduced the aircraft's fuel load so much that its range was only 170 miles.

Franklin D Roosevelt, president of a neutral USA while Nazi armies rapidly overran Europe from September 1939, regarded American military air power as 'utterly inadequate' compared with the advanced might of Germany. He resolved to support the Allied cause in Europe without direct military involvement, and large numbers of fighters and bombers were seen as the only feasible response to such apparently unstoppable aggression. As America slowly recovered from the Great Depression, Roosevelt advocated many new factories to build military equipment.

In June 1941 the Führer launched his invasion of the Soviet Union, and although the Royal Air Force had held off the Luftwaffe in the Battle of Britain the previous year, the German threat remained if the USSR was defeated. If Britain also fell, the Americans would be unable to base bombers in England in order to prevent Hitler from grabbing the resources of Soviet Russia. Operating bombers from the USA would then become the only option, and no existing aircraft could meet that requirement. However, Britain stood strong following America's entry into World War 2, and England duly became a 'terrestrial aircraft carrier' for a massive USAAF offensive against German-occupied Europe from the summer of 1942.

The mile-long production facility of Plant 4 at 'Cowtown', Texas, was devoted to B-24 mass production for that purpose, which in turn meant that the intercontinental bomber project had to wait. Once the Eighth Air Force's British airfields were secured, there was no need to prioritise funding for another complex new bomber since the B-29 was already being developed in great secrecy. However, an intensive high-priority research programme was instigated for the B-36 as a long-term, vital strategic asset, overseen by I M 'Mac' Laddon, executive vice-president and chief engineer at the Consolidated Aircraft Corporation.

BOMBER LOGIC

The use of strategic bombers during World War 2 seemed to prove the theories of Col Billy Mitchell and Gen Giulio Douhet expressed in the 1920s that 'the bomber will always get through', albeit at considerable cost. The most advanced strategic bomber of the conflict was the B-29, which commenced operations in June 1944. With its 3000-mile range and atomic

YB-36 42-13571 initially had the single-wheel main landing gear that was subsequently replaced both on the XB-36 and on this aircraft by multi-wheel units. Evolved during the winter of 1946-47, it had a completely revised flightdeck to accommodate a nose gun turret (*Author's Collection*)

bomb capability (which brought the Pacific War to a terrifying end), the Superfortress seemed to be proof of the strategic bomber's primacy as a decisive weapon.

In March 1946, Strategic Air Command (SAC) was created to ensure peace in a world where only the USA would carry the 'big stick' of a nuclear deterrent. Soviet premier Joseph Stalin made no secret of his desire to expand his empire, and the USSR soon copied the B-29 as the Tupolev Tu-4, giving the Soviet bloc potential nuclear capability. It enabled them to attack any target in Europe or fly one-way missions to the USA.

When it became clear in September 1949 that the USSR also had atomic weapons, the introduction of a more capable, longer-ranging successor to the B-29 became the basis for the creation and massive expansion of SAC's bomber force. By the end of 1949 that force employed 71,500 personnel, owned almost 1000 aircraft and was still expanding rapidly. A year earlier, it had only six crews with training in nuclear delivery and a major problem in retaining relevant manpower, but by the end of 1948 there were 70 crews with atomic weapons training and an intensive recruitment drive was in full swing.

In its ambitious initial 1941 request for a 'very heavy' bomber, the US Army Air Corps (USAAC) specified a range of 12,000 miles at 25,000 ft. It would cruise at 275 mph, but reach a maximum of 450 mph and an absolute ceiling of 45,000 ft. As air-to-air refuelling was still thought impractical, and was never seriously considered for the B-36, the fuel requirements for such long range immediately dictated a massive airframe. By January 1948 attitudes to aerial refuelling had changed. Gen George Kenney, commander of SAC, stated, 'I don't know any project that is more important than the refuelling project right now'. SAC bombers like the B-29 and B-50 (essentially an improved Superfortress) were adapted to use it, but the B-36 remained self-sufficient for fuel.

The aircraft's expanded size also enabled carriage of the enormous 43,000-lb 'earthquake' bomb to blast underground bunkers, as well as the very heavy early nuclear devices such as the Mk 3 'Fat Man' bomb. Initially though, the new intercontinental bomber was conceived as a carrier for 10,000 lbs of conventional ordnance.

Before 1940, the largest bomber projects had been the 35-ton XB-15 (first flown in October 1937) and the XB-19 (first flown in June 1941). Both were one-offs and both were powered by four 1000 hp piston engines. Essentially experimental aircraft with a 212-ft wingspan, they were used to establish the feasibility of heavy bombers with a range of 5000 miles. Their speed, range, engine power and bomb capacity were well below the US War Department's real targets and series production was not intended, although some of the XB-19's systems were used in the B-36.

Instead, Boeing and Consolidated were requested in April 1941 to submit proposals based on their respective Model 384 and six-engined Model 385, together with the 164-ft wingspan Model 35 with four pusher-tractor engines, although none of these projects appeared to be very promising at the time. Boeing, fully occupied with B-17 production, devoted little attention to what they considered an unfeasible project.

In order to ease the designers' tasks, the parameters were revised, reducing the combat radius by 1000 miles to 4000 miles, the maximum range to

10,000 miles and the cruising speed to 240 mph. Service ceiling was cut to 40,000 ft. The choice of six pusher engines was reinforced by the USAAC's Air Materiel Division researchers at the Wright Field Aeronautical Engineering Center in Ohio. As well as minimising drag, the arrangement improved directional stability. Brig Gen George Kenney, heading the USAAF's Experimental Division at Wright Field, promoted the Consolidated proposal to Gen Henry 'Hap' Arnold, Chief of the Army Air Forces, as the most likely to meet these still-challenging targets, partly because its design guidelines appeared to be relatively conventional and risk-free.

Seen in August 1954, John D McEachern and Beryl A Erickson flew most of the early B-36 test flights (*NARA*)

That judgement, however, probably would not have applied to one of the company's alternative design options. Echoing Jack Northrop's contemporary work on the XB-35 flying wing bomber, Consolidated also sketched out an all-wing aircraft with six pusher engines, before reverting to a conventional airframe format with twin vertical stabilisers for its 230-ft wingspan Model 36, reflecting many changes from the Model 35. It had six pusher radial 'Wasp-X' engines and an outline that began to resemble the eventual B-36. After further redesign, two XB-36 experimental aircraft were ordered on 15 November 1941 and a design team led by Harry Sutton and Ted Hall began detailed work on the metal monster.

Northrop's flying wing was an unsolicited entry for the April 1941 competition, and six months later a contract was awarded for initial design work on his XB-35, which was also intended to carry 10,000 lbs of bombs on transatlantic missions to Europe.

Northrop felt that the Air Materiel Center's requirements could be met by a smaller, less complex aircraft than the giant bombers that other manufacturers were promoting. Although his flying wing design was estimated to take longer to develop than an enlarged conventional airframe, he saw it as a simpler project, with such enhanced wing lift and reduced drag and weight that it would require half of the power needed to propel a B-36-sized aircraft. It would also achieve an extra 100 mph. The bomber's wing, spanning 172 ft, was considerably smaller than the Consolidated flying wing sketch, but it would contain everything that had to fit into the fuselage and wing of a B-36-type aircraft.

Like the Consolidated and Boeing designs, the Northrop bomber would continue the 'flying fortress' concept by having formidable defensive armament. Although the futuristic B-35, and its RB-35 reconnaissance bomber variant, were seen for a time as credible rivals, or at least as SAC stablemates to the B-36, the USAF also doubted whether Northrop's production facility would be capable of manufacturing large numbers of the flying wing bombers. Fort Worth's Plant 4, however, was ideal for the task, and the company was told in October 1948 to produce the first 29 B-49As (essentially B-35s modified to use jet engines) alongside a run of 100 B-36s there. Sutton had doubts about the flying wing's inherent stability and control, but the company maintained an interest in the idea, although it was not pursued for any Consolidated design.

By November 1948 it was clear that Gen Curtis LeMay, who had succeeded Kenney as commander of SAC the previous month, favoured the B-36 over the Northrop aircraft. He also envisaged the swept-wing, jet-powered B-47 Stratojet entering service in 1951 (the same in-service date as the RB-49), and performing the medium bomber mission more effectively than the flying wing. A spate of defence project cancellations at the end of 1948 was an opportunity to include the RB-49, and use some of the savings to increase advance orders for the B-36.

Throughout the flying wing's gestation, the aircraft had suffered from persistent problems with the engine transmission systems for the four twin pusher propellers on its wing trailing edge. More seriously, in the absence of modern computers that can make a tailless aircraft sufficiently stable in flight, the XB-35 exhibited real and potential control problems that provided SAC with more reasons to cancel both it and its jet-powered successor, the B/RB-49, which was capable of 500 mph, but lacked the internal space for a large nuclear weapon.

Jack Northrop's troubled flying wing was finally brought down in January 1949, although its basic concept would re-emerge 30 years later with projects leading to the B-2A Spirit. The latter would feature technology that solved the control difficulties associated with the flying wing, and also make the B-36 seem as primitive as the 'Barling Bomber' would have looked in the era of the 'Peacemaker'.

B-36A-1 44-92004 was the first production example completed by Consolidated. After its first flight, on 28 August 1947, the bomber was flown to Wright Field three days later by Col Thomas Gerrity and B A Erickson and suspended in a structural loads airframe for destructive testing after just 7.5 hours of flying time (*Author's Collection*)

CHAPTER TWO

BIRTH OF A HEAVYWEIGHT

With more than 40,000 employees and 13 divisions in various parts of the USA, Consolidated was seen as well placed to take on a major project like the XB-36. It became a massive organisation that would in time evolve into General Dynamics and survive until 1995. The company also had the advantage of running the world's largest aircraft factory at the windowless Plant 4.

The two XB-36 prototypes were to be delivered in May and December 1944, three years after the initial contract. In that time the company had to grapple with the difficulties of producing such a colossal airframe with little available research data to calculate the relevant structural parameters. The basis was a high-mounted wing spanning 230 ft with an area of 4772 sq ft, more than four times the area of the previous Consolidated big bomber, the B-24. The fuselage was a cylindrical structure 163 ft in length, and a twin vertical tail unit (a Convair 'trademark') was carried over from the earlier Model 35. In its production version, the fuselage's length ahead of the wing would make it develop a 'whipping' action in turbulent air, causing discomfort for the crew.

The designers' main challenges stemmed from the 10,000-mile range requirement carrying up to 40 tons of bombs. Their bomber would have to stay aloft for nearly two days, and it would need engines that were sufficiently reliable to sustain a flight of that length and enough crew to operate the bomber for that time, allowing for fatigue and replacement

B-36A-15 44-92022 overflies Lowry AFB, Colorado, which trained B-29 crews from 1943 and became the base for SAC's 3415th Technical Training Wing from 1948. This aircraft was one of 22 B-36As (and the YB-36) that were rebuilt as RB-36E reconnaissance bombers (*Terry Panopalis Collection*)

crews to cover rest periods. Although the aircraft's gross weight would exceed 266,000 lbs, the quest for weight reduction continued throughout its development, as did efforts to reduce drag to a minimum. Wind tunnel tests showed that a NACA 63 aerofoil was preferred, with three degrees of sweepback.

Providing space for six fuel tanks holding 21,116 US gallons, together with the positioning of the engine installations and their cooling requirements, dictated a thick wing, as did the need to be able to access the engines internally for maintenance during the exceptionally long flights. Two more auxiliary tanks, each holding 4788-US-gallon, were located in the wing root area and a single 2996-US-gallon tank occupied a centre fuselage bomb-bay space. An additional 3000-US-gallon tank could be installed in the third bomb-bay and another in the No 2 bay of some aircraft, giving a total fuel load ten times that of a B-17 from World War 2.

The wing tanks were conventional self-sealing rubber types, but evolutionary weight increases in the XB-36 prototype necessitated their replacement by integral tanks with rubber panels on their lower surfaces to provide a self-sealing element. They occupied six sealed compartments between the front and rear wing spars. Internal sealing to prevent frequent leaks took three years to develop, and the problem was eventually solved by using Proseal rubber sealant on the interior surfaces of all the tanks.

Tanks had to be filled individually, and dipsticks (seven-foot wooden poles marked in increments of 100 or 200 gallons) were inserted to check fuel levels. The float/lever type fuel gauges were not very accurate, and they were replaced by electronic gauges from the B-36F onwards. Oil tanks, one for each engine, were checked in the same way to help in the calculation of take-off weight. When the XB-36 first flew it carried only 8000 gallons of fuel, and the oil tanks held a total of 600 gallons.

METALLIC INNOVATIONS

In order to avoid the need for many thousands of rivets for the aircraft's skin, and also in an effort to reduce aerodynamic drag, Consolidated developed strong adhesives to glue the metal panels in place. The bonding was also available in tape form, and it was used to affix about a third of the exterior panels, particularly the magnesium areas. This bonding had better fatigue resistance than riveting, and it was one of the generally useful innovations created for the B-36.

The wing's depth at its root was 7.5 ft, allowing an engineer to enter and work inside it in flight. This became one of the B-36's many sources of public amazement at its sheer size. In action, crew members hauled themselves along a crawl-way that passed over the wheel wells and above the inner engines in order to do limited in-flight engine monitoring and maintenance. At altitude, this meant wearing oxygen masks in these unpressurised spaces and surviving extremely low temperatures. Among the other 'biggest-and-most' superlatives circulated about the B-36 was the fact that it contained 27 miles of electrical wiring.

Another of the design's distinctive features was the extensive and innovative use of magnesium in the structure, making the programme the most important large-scale user of the metal at the time. More easily available than aluminium, although more expensive, it formed the outer skin on around half of the fuselage, the control surfaces (which were originally covered in doped fabric on the B-36A/B variants), the rear section of the wing and engine nacelles and the front portion of the vertical stabiliser. Pressurised areas of the front and rear fuselage had aluminium skin, which was better able to cope with changes in internal pressure. Magnesium was also used for many fittings such as air ducts and bellcranks in the control systems.

An 80-ft-long pressurised tube, similar to the one in the B-29, connected the pressurised forward fuselage crew compartments with the aft compartment, which contained the toilet (for up to 16 crew members), galley and four or six rest bunks for the prolonged flights. Crew members had to lie on their backs on a small, four-wheeled trolley, carrying a chest parachute, and pull themselves along hand over hand using a rope attached to the ceiling of this unpopular communications tube. It was only 25 inches wide and unlit, apart from two small windows to inspect the bomb-bay. Hatches at each end had to be opened externally to maintain pressurisation in the tube.

Turbulent air conditions or darkness would have been further disincentives to making the journey, and depressurisation of the tube was always a possibility. Rather than make this claustrophobic trip to the rear bunks (where engine noise was even louder than in the forward compartment, and it was also possible to feel the rear fuselage flexing disconcertingly from side to side in flight), the flightdeck crew often preferred to cat-nap in their seats or in two temporary bunks in the navigator's area and the relatively spacious radio compartment for aircraft from the B-36D onwards.

One crew member, often the third pilot doubling as a forward gunner, had the task of taking hot meals from the galley along this 'sled ride' for the flightdeck crew. The food could also be sent in specially designed containers, and the trolley was then controlled with a rotating handle to operate its pulley system. A hand brake was provided on the side of the 'sled' to avoid overshoots on a downward journey when the aircraft was climbing to cruise altitude. Even so, crews found the aircraft generally more comfortable than their previous B-29s although the addition of more crew in the RB-36 versions, taking the total beyond 22, left little space.

POWER BY PRATT & WHITNEY

Selection of appropriate engines was obviously crucial and the new, unproven Pratt & Whitney 28-cylinder 'X-Wasp', later known as the R-4360 Wasp Major, was the most advanced piston engine available, and the only suitable one for the project. It was still in the early design

Test pilot John D McEachern takes to the crew communications tunnel – dubbed the 'tube' – at Carswell on 24 April 1949. Crew members lying on the cart for the 85-ft journey between the front and rear compartments used an overhead rope to pull themselves along, hastened by asking the pilot to raise or lower the aircraft's nose slightly. Oxygen masks, parachutes and emergency oxygen bottles were carried in case of explosive decompression (*Terry Panopalis Collection*)

OPPOSITE
The 110-inch diameter wheel used for the XB-36, YB-36 and the XC-99 transport derivative. Beryl Erickson recalled that it took a specialised crew several days to fit one tyre, but they lasted for up to 75 landings on the two bomber versions (*Terry Panopalis Collection*)

stage in 1941, combining two 14-cylinder Twin Wasp engines to produce 3000 hp. In later versions it developed an unprecedented 3800 hp, and the R-4360 became the powerplant for a series of other large aircraft including the B-50, KC-97, C-119 and C-124.

The engine's complex hydraulic, fuel transfer and propeller control systems would provide many maintenance challenges throughout the B-36's service life, while numerous engine fires occurred. Pratt & Whitney and Ford manufactured 18,697 R-4360s, with General Electric BH-2 turbosuperchargers being fitted to the B-36 engines in order to maintain their sea-level performance at high altitudes.

Positioning six complex R-4360s in the rear of a B-36's wing created smooth airflow over the latter, but it also resulted in major cooling problems compared with a conventional location with the engines facing forwards. The engine fires that plagued the B-36 were at least less serious than fires in engines placed at the front of a wing, where they would burn through the structure. In some

Maintainers at Ramey AFB tend to the R-4360 engines of a 72nd SRW aircraft in May 1956. B-36 models had propeller blades that were heated with hot air to prevent icing. Square-tipped blades were usually fitted to engines with fuel injection systems (*Terry Panopalis Collection*)

cases, blazing engines burned out and even fell away from the B-36's wing without seriously endangering the aircraft. Convair developed an innovative methyl-bromide fire extinguisher system in place of the usual carbon dioxide type. A large fan was placed in the cooling air duct ahead of each eight-foot-long engine, but overheating remained a problem at high altitude and full power.

Three-bladed reversing propellers, 19 ft in diameter, were used, originally with rounded tips. There was concern that the low-frequency vibration and buffeting from the inboard propellers could damage the adjacent fuselage sides and the horizontal stabiliser, so four-bladed propellers of 16-ft diameter were test-flown, but not adopted. In service use, pilots often shut down the two inboard engines as the B-36 could cruise on four engines. Buffeting was eventually reduced from 1952 by using square-tipped 'high altitude' blades with reduced pitch.

Each engine in its basic form weighed 3670 lbs – an initial worry to Convair designers who were hoping for lighter options. They comprised a third of the aircraft's empty weight, and the heavier weight of the production versions reduced speed and

altitude figures, and also left the aircraft short of its intended 10,000-mile range. The engines required their own oil tanks close to them in the outer wing panels, and oil leaks were common in versions prior to the R-4360-53 (used from the B-36F onwards) due to leaky rocker covers in the engines.

Devising landing gear that would support the aircraft's 410,000-lb maximum weight also needed super-size solutions. As multi-wheel undercarriage members with appropriate braking systems had not yet been developed, and each main gear member had to retract into the wing, the designers chose a single-wheel type which would fit the available wing space. It required the largest aircraft tyres ever made. Goodyear manufactured the 110-inch diameter, 1,475-lb tyres with 225-lb inner tubes inflated to 100 psi. They fitted 850-lb wheels with additional 750-lb multiple-disc brakes (unavailable until 1948), bringing the total weight of each main gear unit to 8550 lbs – the approximate loaded weight of a P-51 Mustang fighter. Fitting a new tyre during early test flights was the work of several days, requiring the use of a giant wrench more than four feet long. Fortunately, a set lasted for 75 of the early test flights.

The four-wheel main landing gear unit of production B-36s and its complex maintenance access equipment. Despite the unit's strength, the left main landing gear strut of a B-36 from the 326th BS/92nd BW fractured as the brakes were released for take-off, penetrating the wing's fuel tanks. The aircraft cartwheeled horizontally, dragging its jet engines, which exploded. The propellers flew off and fuel flowed towards the fire, but the crew escaped unharmed (*Terry Panopalis Collection*)

Apart from the potentially dire consequences of a tyre failure, with so much weight concentrated on a single tyre's contact surface, there were only three runways strong enough to support the aircraft without cracking – Fort Worth, Eglin AFB in Florida and the facility that became Travis AFB in California.

Faced with a similar problem, the Brabazon's designers opted for twin five-foot diameter tyres to spread the load. By 1945, Consolidated had been directed by the USAAF to develop a new type of multi-wheel undercarriage system, initially using twin wheels like the B-29. This made only small improvements in weight distribution, so a four-wheel bogie unit was designed, using 56-inch diameter tyres and a sophisticated new braking system. It was duly fitted to production B-36As and later models, with a bulge in the wing surfaces to accommodate the landing gear's greater width. The new undercarriage meant the aircraft could now operate from any SAC-capable airfield.

Powering such a massive undercarriage exceeded the capability of the industry-standard 1500 psi hydraulic system. Consolidated, therefore, had to produce a new, lighter system operating at 3000 psi, and this became standard for aircraft until the 1990s. Lightweight electrical systems were used for the six-section flaps, with electro-mechanical synchronisers to coordinate their movement.

ARMAMENT

The B-36's 163-ft-long fuselage was given four bomb-bays for a maximum load of 72,000 lbs, including up to 67 different types of conventional and varied ordnance. The forward and aft bays (Nos 1 and 4) were each designed for 38 500-lb general purpose bombs, or 19 1000-lb versions on 15 different types of rack, arranged vertically inside the bays. Eight 2000-lb or three 4000-lb bombs could be loaded instead.

Bulkheads between bays 1 and 4 and central bays 2 and 3 could be moved to the side by electric motors so that the combined bays could each accommodate two 12,000-lb weapons, two 22,000-lb T-14 Grand Slam bombs stacked vertically or a 43,000-lb 26-ft-long T-12 blockbuster. Different suspension methods involving slings were fitted for the very large ordnance types. Electrically operated doors slid up the sides of the bays, rather like those of the B-24 in principle, but they were later replaced by more rapidly opening hydraulic doors.

The total weight of bombs exceeded that of the heaviest Vietnam-era B-52D Stratofortresses by 26,000 lbs, and equalled the combat weight of two loaded B-25 Mitchell medium bombers.

The bomb-bays were also designed for the massive first-generation US nuclear weapons, including the Mk 3 'Fat Man' and Mk 4 – a massive device more than ten feet long and five feet in diameter, weighing 10,800 lbs. These bombs were too large for the weapons bays of the XB-35, which was one of the reasons for the B-36's selection by SAC rather than the 'flying wing' bombers which were conceived around conventional bomb loads.

Some of the early weapons, including the 15.25-ft-long Mk 7, were also too large for the B-50 to hold, whereas the B-36 could carry any US nuclear bomb. Its disadvantages such as relatively low speed and the limited number of airfields from which the bomber could operate were accepted in the USAAF's September 1945 assessment that it was the only American bomber suitable for long-range nuclear delivery. As the weight and size of the 11 types of weapon were progressively changed, the B-36's bomb-bay fittings, such as sway braces and suspension points, had to be repeatedly modified in Project On Top until a universal bomb suspension (UBS) system could be developed in 1952.

When thermonuclear (hydrogen) bombs entered the US inventory, their size meant that the B-36 was the only bomber able to carry them for two years until 1955, when the B-52 was available. The early designs for this Armageddon device included weight of 50,000 lbs and a 20-ft length. From November 1953, 108 B-36s were modified to carry these Mk 14 and Mk 17 weapons, and this number was later increased to 219, together with the RB-36 fleet. The 24.7-ft-long Mk 17 'Runt' was the largest hydrogen bomb in the armoury, weighing 42,000 lbs and capable of carriage only by the B-36. It was tested in Operation *Castle* in 1954, when crews found that their aircraft suddenly gained up to 1000 ft in altitude as the Mk 17's immense burden was released.

'Runts' were involved in several potentially disastrous incidents with B-36s, including a Biggs AFB aircraft which was transporting a Mk 17 from Texas to Kirtland AFB, New Mexico, on 22 May 1957. The weapon was normally locked into place in the bomb-bay by a shackle, which had to be removed before landing. This was done on approach to Kirtland, but an electrical fault, and a crewman inadvertently leaning on a crucial switch, released the weapon, which crashed through the closed bomb-doors and landed four miles from the base control tower. Fortunately, the weapon was unarmed, and it was destroyed by its own internal high explosives, creating a 12-ft crater but very little radiation leakage. The only victim was a cow.

In 1941 it was considered essential for the B-36, like its predecessors, to have very heavy defensive armament. It continued the tradition established for the B-17 and its contemporaries of multiple turrets giving full hemispherical coverage. The faster bombers that would succeed the B-36 would restrict their defences to radar-operated tail guns as additional weapons were eventually replaced by more sophisticated electronic countermeasures devices.

In Project Featherweight in 1954, the B-36 would also sacrifice all but its tail guns to achieve greater speed and altitude, high altitude being the bomber's principal defence against fighters. Early B-36 designs included sufficient armament to tackle three interceptors attacking simultaneously. The 'Hometown' defensive formation was later devised so that a cell of three B-36s could provide optimum mutual defence against fighter attack from the rear.

One early specification was for ten 0.50-cal machine guns possibly in four-gun turrets, with a 37 mm cannon added to the twin 'fifties' in the tail position, two 37 mm guns in an upper turret and two more in a retractable turret below the forward fuselage. Such comprehensive coverage would have given the bomber the defensive capability of a medium-calibre, terrestrial anti-aircraft battery. A 1942 Armament Review advocated replacing the 0.50-cal guns with even heavier 0.60-cal weapons in twin-gun turrets.

The agreed armament for early-production B-36s consisted of eight remote-controlled turrets in unpressurised compartments, each with twin 20 mm M24A1 or M24E2 lightweight cannons firing at 600 or 700 rounds per minute. Fixed turrets were located in the nose and tail and six fully retractable, electrically operated D-1 turrets were positioned above the forward and rear fuselage, with D-2 turrets in the lower forward and rear fuselage positions.

In order to reach the required performance targets it was essential to make the turrets retractable to reduce drag. The combined 2400- to 2880-lb weight of the armament, far in excess of the original specification, together with parasitic drag from their individual bulged observation blisters reduced top speed by 8 mph, although this was in part due to drag from the enlarged contours of the tail turret. Yet another pair of turrets was originally planned to fire from below the forward fuselage, but its place was taken on production B-36s by AN/APS-13 and AN/APQ-23 search radar, replacing the AN/APG-7 Eagle system that had originally been specified.

The first version of the B-1 fire control system was derived from the General Electric A-1 under development for the B-29, but in 1946 it was found that it interfered with the aircraft's other electronics, requiring months of trouble shooting. At one stage the B-1's problems

The rear upper guns of a Ramey AFB-based RB-36 in the retracted position. The upper and lower turrets were five feet high, although little of them protruded above the surface of the aircraft when extended. Firing the guns caused noise and vibration throughout the bomber (*Terry Panopalis Collection*)

almost precipitated its removal and replacement by manually operated 0.50-cal turrets.

Each turret had a gunner, which meant that eight of the typical 15-man crew manned weapons. Several of them also had other duties to perform, including observation, assistance for radar and navigation or as second radio operators. For most missions they were unlikely to encounter fighters at the B-36's operational altitudes, and the turrets remained in the retracted position, covered by quick-acting flush doors. Extended, they obviously created drag at a time when the bomber needed all the speed it could generate.

The gunners sat in remote sighting positions, one to each turret, controlling the guns with several types of General Electric sighting system, each one linked to a single turret rather than being transferrable to control other turrets as in the B-29. Seven were visually controlled, and the tail guns were aimed by radar. Crew sitting in position near a blister had to attach themselves to the aircraft with a safety strap in case the Perspex bubble became damaged, causing sudden decompression.

The four upper fuselage systems used 'yoke' sights with light-weight fire control computers and vacuum tube thyratron controllers, mounted in transparent blisters close to the guns they controlled. The gunner moved the entire sight, viewing the target as a fighter pilot would through a small transparent plate that provided an aiming dot and a circle of dots that could be set to match the wingspan of an attacking fighter. He then had to track his target, firing through an arc that extended 100 degrees forward and aft in azimuth and from 24 degrees below and 89 degrees above horizontal, with fire interrupters to avoid self-harm to the aircraft. The sights were equipped with 16 mm Bell & Howell gun cameras.

The gunners sat back to back in positions reminiscent of wartime B-17s but in far more comfortable conditions, aiming gunsights through transparencies rather than bucking, blazing 0.50-cal guns through open windows. The 5000 rounds of 20 mm ammunition had to be loaded into belts from boxes next to the aircraft and carried up ladders into the turrets.

The lower sighting blisters had pedestal-mounted sights developed from the type used in the B-29. They worked in a similar way to yoke sights, and controlled firing through almost the same parameters in the aircraft's lower hemisphere. They had a single eyepiece, rather than the periscopic double-prism of the yoke sight which gave a wider view. All the sighting stations had basic ring-and-bead back-up sights in case the electronics malfunctioned.

A rearward-facing gunner in the aft pressurised compartment controlled the tail guns using an AN/APG-3, with a single radome beneath the rudder housing a gun-laying

The upper forward turrets were often extended just before landing to provide a useful escape route in the event of an emergency. They weighed more than 700 lbs each. Spent cartridges and links from the upper turrets were collected in canvas bags (*USAF*)

radar with a similar thyratron controller and computer to the other positions. The turret was almost spherical, and covered a 60-degree cone of fire. An AN/APG-3 could track and lock on to a target at a range of 4.5 miles. The later AN/APG-32 in the B-36D or AN/APG-41 with twin scanners and radomes could track one target while searching for a second with the other radar.

The tail turret of a B-36H-10 (like 51-15705 of the 7th BW seen here) boasted two M24A1 20 mm cannon that could fire between 550 and 820 rounds per minute, although a rate of 600 rounds per minute was usually selected. It was aimed with the twin-radome AN/APG-41 by a gunner in the rear compartment, the weapons firing M96 incendiary, M97 high-explosive or AP-1 armour-piercing projectiles (*Terry Panopalis Collection*)

The original XB-36 design omitted a nose turret, but wartime experience of deadly head-on attacks by Luftwaffe fighters brought about a redesign for production aircraft. Twin 20 mm guns were mounted in a non-retractable turret, with a hemispheric sight using a single eyepiece that allowed the gunner to see targets within a field of vision that extended 90 degrees up, down or sideways. Its 20 mm ammunition was fed from two 400-round boxes, while the other turrets used two 600-round boxes each.

When it became apparent that the Soviet Union was developing fighters that could reach the B-36's altitude, it was thought that high-speed head-on attacks would be the least likely form of fighter interception. The nose turret was therefore the most obvious one to remove during the weight reductions programmes that affected late B-36 models.

All the turret compartments were accessible in flight if the crew compartments were first depressurised, and in an emergency their hatches could be opened to allow escape from the aircraft on the ground.

The gunners had their own separate intercom system to coordinate their firepower. During the Korean War, B-29 gunners, flying at much lower altitudes than the B-36s, found that their sighting systems were often too slow in operation to track MiG-15 jet interceptors with their 0.50-cal guns. B-36 gunners would never have the opportunity to test their systems or their heavier weapons in action. Instead, at their much higher altitudes they had to cope with the difficulties of operating the guns in -67°F temperatures. The guns had heaters to prevent their lubricating oil from freezing, but the whole system worked much better at lower altitudes.

In training, two- to three-second bursts were recommended, with a 60-second cooling pause between them (with the turret turned into the airstream) to minimise barrel wear and prevent rounds from 'cooking off'.

Debates about the B-36's defensive weaponry would continue throughout the bomber's development, and it was one of the most troublesome aspects of the aircraft's operational life as the demands for increased performance multiplied, culminating in the guns' removal by March 1955 in the Featherweight programme. The crew was reduced by up to five when all but the tail guns were sacrificed in Featherweight III.

DEFINING THE MONSTER

Airframe development continued, including progressive weight increases, throughout 1945, with a significant change in July. Based on static tests, the USAAF considered that the double vertical stabilisers could easily be damaged in turbulent air conditions or a heavy landing. They were then replaced in the design by a single vertical stabiliser that topped out at 47 ft above the ground, reduced drag and saved 3850 lbs of weight. Its rudder had no static lock and was vulnerable to strong winds on the ground. The company's B-32 Dominator bomber, designed for use from bases in the Marianas as a partner to the B-29 in the war against Japan, was similarly redesigned with a single tail fin in 1945.

The B-36's conventional flying controls, with mechanical linkages, relied on servo tab operation in the absence of powered boosting. The elevators were forced up and down aerodynamically by trim tabs, not hydraulics. Pilots were surprised at the ease with which they could control the bomber despite its size, until supplementary jet engines were hung under the outer wings later in its career. After that addition, the co-pilot often had to supply some extra muscle to manage the ailerons. However, the B-36 was considered unusually stable in flight compared with other contemporary large aircraft with reciprocating engines, even though control responses were quite slow. They allowed the pilot very little 'feel' and required anticipation of control application. Formation flying required considerable effort.

Manoeuvrability of the early versions of the 178-ton aircraft at high altitude was considered good enough to evade any fighters, and pilots found the control forces were light on take-off and landing. The tall tail and considerable wing area did cause difficulty in crosswind take-offs and landings, particularly in moving the rudder. In normal conditions, at least one pilot proved that it was quite possible to fly and land the aircraft despite having lost the rudder during a sortie. Maj George Keller even managed to land a B-36 with the ailerons jammed in the neutral position.

Instrumentation for the pilots remained fairly similar throughout early B-36 models, such as this RB-36D-15 (49-2696). For the B-36H/J, the jet engines' instruments were integrated into the main panel, rather than being on two separate panels either side of the throttles as seen here. Jet controls remained on an overhead panel (*Terry Panopalis Collection*)

Taxiing accurately was challenging as the pilot was sitting 80 ft ahead of the main landing gear, but the domed cockpit canopy gave him good all-round visibility, despite its network of framing. The cockpit area, however, was crowded and cramped, although the pressurised crew compartments offered more comfort than others of that era, where oxygen masks were necessary.

Consolidated Vultee had an XB-36 mock-up completed in San Diego for USAAF inspection by 20 July 1942. Despite the shortfalls in performance due to increased weight, the mock-up was approved two months later. Permission was also given on 6 August to produce the aircraft at the Fort Worth plant, completed in January 1942, rather than in the company's main San Diego facility.

Consolidated argued that commencing production straight away alongside the flight-testing schedule, before construction of the prototype had even begun, would enable its bomber to enter service two years earlier than would have been the case if the usual process of prototype testing was adhered to. The USAAF, however, preferred to see Consolidated focusing on turning out more B-24s for the war effort, together with its immediate successor, the B-32 Dominator. This enlarged B-24-derived bomber, with remote-controlled gun turrets, briefly entered service in the last few months of the Pacific War, mainly as insurance against the failure of the B-29, but it was cancelled the day after the Japanese surrender and all incomplete airframes from the order for 114 B-32s were scrapped at Plant 4.

There was a change of policy in July 1943 when the Secretary of War, Henry Stimson, judged that use of the B-36 from bases in Alaska or Hawaii might shorten the fight against Japan. The alternative was to wait until the Mariana Islands were won back at huge cost in American lives so that they could be used as bases for the shorter-ranged B-29 or B-24. Even though the Marianas were re-occupied by late 1944, the USAAF's comparatively modest order for 100 B-36s was signed on 19 August 1944, with deliveries to begin a year later, on the assumption that the war might continue until 1947. This contract survived the end of the war in Europe, as the Pacific scenario was still thought to require much longer-ranging aircraft than those that had defeated Hitler.

As manufacture of the XB-36 (42-13570, with the 'buzz' number BM-570) continued at a slow pace at Fort Worth, the USAAF had to take account of the performance reductions from its specified statistics for their forthcoming heavyweight. Estimated maximum speed was now 323 mph, a loss of 46 mph. Service ceiling was 38,200 ft, rather than 40,000 ft, and, crucially, 640 miles were cut from the intended 10,000-mile range. At the root of these reductions was a 13,000-lb weight increase since development had commenced, taking the bomber's total weight to in excess of 124 tons. This included more than five tons of extra armament weight necessitated by a change to twin 20 mm cannon in fully retractable turrets (in addition to the nose and tail turrets, which were non-retractable) specified by the USAAF. Also, the crew was increased in size to 14.

Even so, a B-36 would be able to exceed the B-29's bomb-carrying ability over a range of 5500 miles by a factor of ten at roughly the same speed. The actual cost of re-taking islands like Iwo Jima and the Marianas, which some historians felt could have been avoided by introducing the B-36 earlier, together with the introduction of atomic weapons, lent more urgency to the acquisition of intercontinental bombers for the future.

Roll-out of the XB-36 missed the Japanese surrender in August 1945 by three weeks. After outfitting and ground tests, it was ready to fly by 8 August 1946 as the largest, heaviest military aircraft ever to take flight, although its delayed development had already occupied more than four-and-a-half years. Shortages of parts and delays caused by labour union strikes had contributed to the hold-ups. The production R-4360-25 engines had arrived by November 1945, and in ground tests and taxi trials beginning on 21 July 1946 their combined propeller turbulence caused the aircraft's fabric-covered flaps to fall apart. There was a six-week delay while new, but much heavier aluminium flaps were fitted.

IT FLIES

For the first flight at 1010 hrs on 8 August 1946, Consolidated test pilot Beryl A Erickson, who had worked on the project for two years and had previously flown the XB-19, took the controls with co-pilot G S 'Gus' Green, who was in overall charge of the flight test programme. The take-off was watched by more than 7000 Fort Worth employees. The XB-36 was airborne for 37 minutes, reaching a modest 155 mph at 3500 ft. The only problem experienced by the crew was the failure of one of the six flaps to retract. Erickson reported that 'the aircraft handled very nicely, despite its size. There were no worrisome surprises'.

Difficulties did arise, however, as the tests continued into the autumn of 1946. These were mainly concerned with engine cooling and vibration from the propellers. Cooling was essential for sustained flight at high altitudes, and several types of two-speed fan were developed to reduce overheating. The vibration issue was mainly a result of placing the big propellers in the aircraft's wing wake, where the turbulence had a greater effect on them and on the flaps, engines and their 'power egg' cowlings than wind tunnel tests had suggested. Remedies for both problems would tax company engineers for several years.

B-36A/Bs would spend an unusually large proportion of their careers in deep maintenance or modification programmes. The bomber would also survive five attempts by influential decision makers in the armed forces to have it cancelled altogether.

When the initial order for 100 B-36s was placed during World War 2 conditions, it was stipulated that the funds had to be spent by June 1948 or be re-allocated by Congress to other projects. Another pressure on Consolidated to bring the aircraft up to service standard was the US government's wish to preserve its large, capable workforce at its Fort Worth facility in the post-war years, rather than lose employees to other industries. It was, therefore, vital to have a credible type on the production line, so testing the B-36 had additional urgency, and solutions to problems like propeller vibration needed quick solutions.

The company also had to build a team of suitably qualified designers and engineers, which had been a difficult task in wartime when so many high-priority projects drew them away. By the end of 1944 the B-36 programme was already 18 months behind schedule.

Additional strengthening to resist the propeller instability

Carswell AFB assembled a formation of 15 B-36s for a 'show of strength' demonstration on 14 February 1949. These rare events revealed just how powerful SAC was to potential enemies, and the Soviet Union attempted similar showcase flypasts on special occasions (*Terry Panopalis Collection*)

inevitably added further weight to the affected areas. By August 1947 the maximum altitude possible in the XB-36 with early BM-2 superchargers was 37,000 ft – 3000 ft below the already reduced target figure. Fatigue could also affect the propeller shafts. In one test flight a fatigue-weakened propeller broke off, chopping off a section of wing flap, and in another both inboard wing flaps came away. In a further unintended and, luckily, harmless 'bombing' incident, a 50-lb external airspeed indicator, trailed on a cable 75 ft below the

B-36A-10 44-92015 *City of Fort Worth* was the first 'Peacemaker' delivered to the 492nd BS/7th BW at Carswell on 26 June 1948. Two previous A-models also bore this name, but 44-92015 was officially the 'first B-36 combat plane delivered to SAC'. 492nd BS personnel line up for a SAC inspection prior to the bomber's first flight by a USAF crew on 28 June 1948 (*Terry Panopalis Collection*)

XB-36, fell off and hit a boys' school, destroying a fortunately unoccupied bidet and causing minor injuries to several pupils. Other problems occurred with lightweight aluminium wiring that proved to be weaker than heavier, standard copper versions, causing electrical fires.

The first major incident occurred on 26 March 1947 during take-off for the 16th test flight. As BM-570's undercarriage was almost retracted, the right main landing gear retraction strut's hydraulic cylinder burst, sending a shockwave through the airframe and fracturing the unit's bracing strut where it connected with the wing spar. The massive wheel and main strut extended again, but swung well past the normal 'down' location, crashing into an adjacent engine nacelle. Fuel and hydraulic lines were smashed and fire broke out in the No 4 engine.

Erickson and the flight engineers surveyed the damage from inside the wing and judged that any sort of repair would be impossible in-flight, particularly as the right-hand landing gear had also failed. It seemed likely that the crew would have to bail out and the only XB-36 would be lost, since attempting a landing with a wrecked undercarriage could be potentially catastrophic.

Erickson circled the Fort Worth airfield for more than five hours burning off 7015 gallons of fuel as it could not be dumped. Twelve crewmen bailed out, two by two, through an aft observation blister, sustaining minor injuries as they landed in strong winds. Erickson and Green stayed with the valuable prototype while massive crowds gathered around the base. Erickson then made a gentle touchdown when the winds had abated and the bomber rolled for 5500 ft with the right landing gear holding out and the left unit propped against the damaged nacelle. When it finally came to a halt on grass next to the runway, it was clear that damage had been minimal. The errant aluminium bracing strut was replaced with a steel one and test flights continued.

By June 1948 the XB-36 had the new four-wheel undercarriage and more powerful R-4360-41 engines developing 3500 hp each. By saving the prototype, Erickson had prevented the programme from falling further behind by up to a year.

CHAPTER THREE

TEST AND DEVELOPMENT

In this line-up of 'Peacemakers' at Carswell, B-36A-10 44-92013 appears to have exchanged rudders with B-36A-15 44-92025. Also present are red-tailed B-36B-1s. Many early 7th and 11th BW crews that flew Carswell-based aircraft were Eighth Air Force bomber group veterans from World War 2. The base became the main hub of B-36 activity, and as deliveries built up overcrowding became a problem (*USAF*)

After initial manufacturer's trials, the next stage of testing took place at Wright Field under the auspices of the USAF, established in September 1947. In June 1948, the XB-36 briefly became a training aid for SAC, which was expecting its first production B-36A for the 7th Bombardment Group (BG). Subsequently returned to Fort Worth, the aircraft was tested with another purely experimental landing gear arrangement in 1950.

The Dowty Equipment Corporation, using an idea from tank suspension designer J Walter Christie, developed a track-type landing gear that used pairs of belts running around sets of roller and idler wheels, like a small tank. They were intended to reduce the pressure of the undercarriage on a runway and enable large aircraft to use unimproved airfields.

Dowty's version, with inflated belts, had been successfully tested in an A-20C bomber in 1943, although it weighed three times as much as conventional landing gear. Firestone-built variants were tested in a P-40 fighter and a C-82A transport aircraft, showing that the gear worked well on snow and soft terrain, but not on sand. The B-50A, which entered service four months before the B-36A, was also scheduled to have tracked gear, and in November 1947 the B-36 was proposed as a recipient, although no practical use was foreseen apart from when the aircraft flew from Arctic staging bases.

The XB-36 was chosen for the experimental installation, mainly to test the application of tracked gear across a range of heavy aircraft, including the heaviest. The three complex units, made by the Cleveland Pneumatic Tool Company and the Goodyear Tire and Rubber Company, increased the 16,000-lb weight of the existing landing gear by at least 5000 lbs, but reduced the pressure on the runway from 156 lbs per square inch to just 57 lbs.

Brief taxi tests of the 'roller skates' began on 26 March 1950, but crew members were unnerved by the hideous, high-pitched screeching and vibration associated with the tracks.

By 30 January 1952 the XB-36's brief career as a test bed had come to an end after 30 flights and the aircraft was grounded at Fort Worth, where it was destroyed on the fire dump. The prototype had helped to overcome many of the objections to serial production of the aircraft, clearing the way for the next in the series of what Gen LeMay regarded as his 'interim bombers'. In that context, the B-36 followed the B-29 as a relatively short-term project pending the arrival of the jet-powered B-47 and B-52.

LeMay's influence on Capitol Hill was strong enough to raise the astronomic funding required for this series of weapons, including the still unproven B-36, which many felt was obsolescent before it entered squadron service. To him, there was 'no ultimate weapon', and dollars had to be lavished on constant development of the deterrent. With the B-52, which may well exceed a century in service, that investment may finally pay off.

The experimental track-tread landing gear that the USAAF/USAF hoped would 'effect maximum practicable weight distribution' on standard or unprepared airfields. Taxi trials with the non-retractable units were conducted in March 1950, but development of multi-wheel landing gear units with better brakes curtailed the programme (*Terry Panopalis Collection*)

BUILDING GIANTS

Despite a background of continued calls for cancellation, plans to implement production of the original 100-aircraft batch at the USAAF-owned Forth Worth facility took shape. However, the second aircraft, the single YB-36 (42-13571), had yet to complete service testing. Ready for its first flight on 4 December 1947, the aircraft differed visibly in having a revised flightdeck (created by Henry Dreyfuss Designs of New York) that answered criticisms from Erickson and Green about lack of visibility from the cockpit. A framed bubble canopy was installed, an aft-facing flight engineer's station was built and the AN/APG-3 tail radar was installed for testing. A twin-gun forward-firing nose turret was incorporated, with a Farrand hemisphere sight. Improved turbosuperchargers enabled the YB-36 to out-perform the XB-36, reaching 40,400 ft altitude in its early test flights.

Before the defeat of Japan, Plant 4 was configured to produce B-32 Dominators, but after the termination of that contract in August 1945 the factory was cleared and tooling for the B-36 was created under the supervision of Factory Manager C H White. The assembly line, from component sub-assembly to completion, took up the whole length of the windowless building (almost one mile). The B-36s had to be built without their outer wing panels as the main building was only 200 ft wide. The airframes were then angled at almost 45 degrees for the latter part of their journey, with the outer wings installed from Station 8 onwards, as their full 230-ft span would not otherwise fit inside the walls. For the final stages, the aircraft had to be angled nose-upwards so that the vertical stabiliser would clear the exit from the building.

Flight testing of the YB-36 continued into June 1948, still with the single-wheel main landing gear and with various partial versions of the defensive armament. It was later brought up to B-36A production standard for SAC use and then reconfigured as an RB-36E, completing 1952.5 hours in service before retirement in 1957.

The first production B-36A (44-92004) was flown on 28 August 1947, three months before the YB-36, and displayed at Fort Worth's adjoining Carswell AFB. It bore the 'buzz' number BM-004 and the name *City of Fort Worth*, which had also been displayed on the company's first B-24 Liberator in 1942. The bomber was then delivered to Wright Field, with a minimum of equipment aboard, for 45 structural integrity tests, leading to its destruction after only 7.5 hours of flight time, most of which was required for the flight to Wright Field.

Production B-36As had revised four-wheel main landing gear units, but were otherwise similar to the YB-36. These new landing gear trucks, used on all subsequent models, spread the aircraft's weight more evenly on the ground but did not altogether rule out sinkage into softer tarmac. A 28th Strategic Reconnaissance Wing (SRW) RB-36 visiting the new airport at Billings, Montana, in 1954 settled eight inches into a new parking bay overnight, requiring full power to pull itself clear.

B-36As had four bomb-bays and positions for eight gunners, although no defensive armament was installed. When the A-model entered service, its performance still fell short of the USAF's original specifications. Combat radius with a 10,000-lb bomb load was 3880 miles, falling to 2100 miles with 72,000 lbs of bombs. With the lighter ordnance load, it was claimed that a top speed of 345 mph could be achieved at 31,600 ft, but the advertised service ceiling was only 29,100 ft – far less than the unloaded YB-36 – until enough fuel had been burned off to allow it to add another 10,000 ft in altitude.

B-36A test flights by company pilots established standard long-range mission profiles for early models of the bomber. After an initial 370-mile leg at 5000 ft, they climbed to 10,000 ft and pushed higher to 25,000 ft when they were 30 minutes from the target, maintaining that altitude for the return trip. A 7000-mile flight on 18 May 1948 included dropping 25 2000-lb bombs on a US Navy range at Corpus Christi, Texas, using the AN/APQ-23 bombing-navigation radar. On 30 June a B-36A demonstrated carriage of a 72,000-lb bomb load – the heaviest ever carried by an aircraft.

SAC's 7th Bombardment Wing (BW), located conveniently at Carswell AFB, adjacent to Plant 4, received its first B-36A (44-92015) on 26 June 1948 to begin replacing its B-29s. It was simply taxied across from the factory to the dispersal used by the 492nd Bombardment Squadron (BS). It was subsequently joined by more examples at the rate of one per week.

Each aircraft was adorned with the 'triangle J' tail marking that the 7th BW had previously used on its B-29s. 44-92015 also had a gold City of Fort Worth plaque attached to its nose by Brig Gen Roger Ramey, commander of the Eighth Air Force.

The 7th had been the first USAAC bomb group to be involved in combat during World War 2 when six of its B-17s landed in Hawaii at the height of the attack on Pearl Harbor. Carswell also had connections to World War 2 and Consolidated, being named after B-24 pilot Maj Horace Carswell, who was awarded the Congressional Medal of Honor for a heroic attack on a Japanese convoy in 1944. For its role as the key B-36 base, new enlarged parking ramps were built and the main runway was extended to 12,000 ft.

Due to its location, the B-29-equipped 7th BW had been nominated as the first B-36 operator on 22 March 1948. Technicians from the wing immediately commenced training on the aircraft at Convair, although delivery of the complex bomber to its three squadrons was held up for 12 weeks by ongoing modifications.

The 11th BG (also previously equipped with B-29s), commanded by Lt Col Harry Goldsworthy and boasting a distinguished record in World War 2, became the second frontline operator of the B-36 from 1 December 1948 following its assignment from Northwest Field, on Guam. It provided training in due course for the 28th BW at Rapid City AFB, South Dakota, in 1949.

SAC planned to operate ten B-36 groups, each with three squadrons of six B/RB-36s, but this complement was increased to ten aircraft per squadron in 1948, and 'groups' became 'wings' from December 1950. When the shorter-ranged B-47s entered service in October 1951 in far greater numbers, 45 aircraft were allocated to each wing.

The first production B-36As had 3000-hp R-4360-25 engines and bomb-bays configured for 72,000 lbs of conventional ordnance in four

The third production B-36A-1, 44-92006 was assigned to Wright-Patterson Air Materiel Center during June 1951 for USAF testing. Twenty-two B-36As were built in 1948, with 44-92005 being the first 'operational' example in May of that year. Early B-36As all had the multi-wheel landing gear units (*Terry Panopalis Collection*)

bays (with slow-opening doors), which remained in the design for the B-36B. No defensive armament was mounted apart from tail turrets in some examples, since the other, retracting, gun turrets were then still under development. The bomber's eight temporarily redundant gunners were listed as observers. An AN/APQ-23 bombing-navigation radar was installed, and the aircraft had the new four-wheel main landing gear bogies.

Company test statistics gave the B-36 a combat radius of 3880 miles with a 10,000-lb bomb load and 24,121 gallons of fuel. Its maximum take-off weight was limited to 310,380 lbs, and the full 72,000-lb bomb load reduced its combat radius to 2100 miles. B-36A 44-92005 was the first truly operational example, accepted in May 1948 and sent to Air Proving Ground Command for climatic testing at Eglin AFB in June.

PROVING THE CONCEPT

7th BW pilot Capt Wesley Morris and bombardier Lt Richard Munday flew test missions for Consolidated, including a 14 May 1948 long-range night mission in which 31 500-lb bombs were deposited on the Wilcox Range in Arizona. Company test pilots B A Erickson and A S 'Doc' Witchell continued to prove the bomber's viability with longer flights that same month. A simulated bombing mission with B-36A 44-92013 (weighing 299,619 lbs) carrying 10,000 lbs of bombs and sufficient ballast to equal the weight of the missing defensive armament took 36 hours for a flight of 8062 miles at 223 mph, the aircraft landing back at Carswell with enough fuel for another 500 miles. These flights proved that the B-36A was still unable to hit its original 10,000-mile target range, even with a full fuel load and no bombs.

In their first year of service, B-36s were able to log very few flying hours as many of the aircraft's test programmes were still being completed in the wake of the bomber's initial acceptance by SAC. Despite these shortcomings Consolidated Vultee and SAC initiated a massive publicity campaign for the bomber, and its propaganda effect in the Soviet bloc could be measured by the enormous investment made by the USSR in developing a large, jet-powered interceptor force.

Maj Gen LeMay took over SAC in October 1948, and he found low levels of effectiveness in many areas. His infamous test of the bomber units on 1 January 1949 confirmed his worst fears. Every SAC group was ordered to take part in a simulated mass bombing mission against Wright Field, and they all fell victim to mechanical and electronic failures, engine problems and general lack of experience against a background of adverse weather. As LeMay remarked, 'You might call that just about the darkest night in American aviation history. Not one airplane finished that mission'. His fury was underscored by the explosion of the first Soviet nuclear weapon in that year.

By February 1949 SAC had 22 B-36As on strength with the 7th BG. They were used for training on the type for both air- and groundcrew while Convair continued to work on the bombers' fuel leaks, propeller vibration, engine overheating and electrical failures, among many other teething problems. For pilots used to the B-29, there were many new facets associated with the bomber's size to become familiar with.

For example, due to the length of the fuselage, they found themselves sitting 30 ft above the ground on rotation with the bomber's main landing gear still on the runway.

DEFENDING THE LEVIATHAN

In 1947 the USAF had accepted the central doctrine of strategic bombing, but it was still hesitant, in the post-war period, about the huge effort and expense of introducing the B-36, the logistics to support it and the escort fighters needed to protect the bomber for at least part of its mission. As SAC's first commander when it was established in March 1946, Gen Kenney had recommended the cancellation of the order for 100 B-36s at $2.5m apiece in favour of the shorter-ranged B-50A 'medium' bomber, based on the proven B-29 and using similar R-4360 engines as the B-36. He conceded that a limited number of B-36s might be used as long-endurance anti-submarine patrollers or even as aerial tankers.

This long debate would eventually lead to the acceptance of the B-47 jet bomber, but it would still leave the USAAF without a very long-range heavy bomber. Rival views came from Gen Carl Spaatz, Commanding General of the Army Air Forces, and Brig Gen Nathan Twining, the Fifteenth Air Force commander, who supported the B-36 in the face of a chilling Cold War in Europe and continued communist threats in the Far East. Both men also feared the possibility of a 'nuclear Pearl Harbor' attack by Soviet bombers and the occupation of Western Europe by the Soviet Union's massive land forces. As in World War 2, very long-range air power would be the USA's only way to retaliate. Although Kenney backed down, his criticisms of the B-36 continued, encouraging other opponents of the bomber.

More serious opposition came from the US Navy, which had feared the loss of its naval air forces to the USAAF after President Harry S Truman's 1945 policy of uniting the US armed forces. The US Navy had ordered the AJ Savage, with twin piston engines and one jet unit, to carry the Mk VI atomic bomb.

As the Savage was not available until 1949, the P2V Neptune, with a wingspan of 100 ft, was seen as an interim nuclear bomber. It certainly fulfilled the range requirements. Prototype XP2V-1 *Truculent Turtle* flew 11,235.6 miles from Columbus, Ohio, to Perth, Western Australia, unrefuelled in September 1946. The flight lasted 55 hrs 17 min, creating a record that stood for almost 20 years.

Neptunes were then flown from the flightdeck of USS *Coral Sea* (CV-43) in April 1948. Shortly thereafter, 12 P2V-3Cs were ordered, these aircraft being specially modified to carry the 9000-lb Mk 8

B-36B-10 44-92056 (the 53rd B-36 built) displays its nose 'greenhouse', with the oval-shaped bomb-aiming transparency for the Norden bombsight. This area felt like a super-heated greenhouse to maintainers working in those spaces in the Texan summer heat. Nose guns and the hemispheric sight (to the left of the central, circular transparency) are removed. An antenna for the ARN-58 instrument approach set stands above the nose (*USAF*)

nuclear bomb. Weighing up to 74,000 lbs, these bombers demonstrated the ability to deliver the weapon against targets up to 2200 miles distant from the carrier in several flights during 1949. Although this performance did not seriously rival the USAF's heavy bombers, it showed that a purpose-built attacker like the AJ Savage did present a potential alternative strike capability from Midway-class carriers.

The USAAF's monopoly over the nuclear deterrent, with the B-36 as its centrepiece, also threatened US Navy plans established in 1945 for four supercarriers beginning with the 65,000-ton USS *United States* (CVA-58), primarily armed with 100,000-lb long-range nuclear-capable bombers. CVA-58's keel was laid in April 1948, but the ship was cancelled five days later without consultation with the US Navy on the grounds that it duplicated the USAF's nuclear role.

Defense Secretary Louis A Johnson, who had been a director of the Consolidated Aircraft Corporation from 1942, had also reduced other aspects of naval power to save money, whereas his predecessor (until March 1949) James V Forrestal had received Congressional funding for balanced US forces including USAF nuclear bombers and CVA-58 for the US Navy. Forrestal and Secretary of the Navy John Sullivan fought to stop the B-36 despite strong Congressional opposition. The strain on Forrestal eventually contributed to his mental breakdown and suicide.

A bitter inter-service struggle continued, inflamed by many published articles and unfounded claims by the US Navy that the B-36 contract was the result of financial incentives to several influential Congressmen by Consolidated Vultee. Adm Arthur Radford, one of the many opponents of the B-36 (he called it the 'billion dollar blunder' and a '1941 airplane'), was the US Navy's spokesman at the October 1949 committee hearings at which the US Navy case was argued.

Disputing the USAF's claims regarding the bomber's survivability, he asserted that Soviet forces would easily be able to intercept it within five years. He advocated smaller, faster tactical bombers such as the US Navy's planned Model 593-8 (XA3D-1 Skywarrior), although they would have attacked targets that suited naval objectives rather than the urban strategic targets that SAC would have tackled. It was accepted that smaller aircraft than the B-36 would have to fly one-way nuclear delivery missions, although their higher speed might at least allow them to reach a target without being intercepted.

To challenge the B-36's survivability, the US Navy proposed test interceptions on the aircraft by its new F2H-2 Banshee fighter. Simulated interceptions using another Banshee as a B-36 substitute at 45,000 ft had revealed that the fighter could bring its 20 mm guns to bear on a high-flying bomber, and also manoeuvre at that altitude. US Navy F9F Panther pilots reported that the bomber filled their gunsights at a range of one mile. McDonnell had intended to fit afterburners to the Banshee, enabling it to reach 40,000 ft within three minutes, but the afterburner installation was cancelled.

The Joint Chiefs of Staff bowed to USAF pressure and refused to allow actual interception tests in case the B-36 was shown to be too vulnerable in daylight attacks against targets with good ground-controlled radar systems. Many years later, Gen LeMay recollected that he had told the Secretary of Defense that the only way to solve the Banshee versus B-36 argument was for the fighter to fire live ammunition at a bomber flown by LeMay himself. His real point was that a simulated interception exercise would have been impractical since actual wartime combat was the only definitive way of evaluating a new weapon.

However, in unofficial practice interceptions of B-36s by US Navy fighters at high altitudes, it was found that shallow turns were sufficient to enable the bomber, with far greater wing area than any fighter, to evade many fighters that struggled to manoeuvre in the thin air. The bomber had to maintain maximum speed. The B-36 was known for slow-acting flight controls and engine acceleration responses, and it could lose speed rapidly if the throttles were cut and the huge drag of the propellers took effect.

For the defence, as Rear Adm Don Engen later stated; 'The Air Force made great pronouncements about the B-36. It was going to do away with the need for fighters. No fighter could fly in the wake of a B-36 without its wings coming off because of the turbulence of the props and jets. We were tasked to go up and show that the wings wouldn't come off the airplane. So, we would use the ship's CIC [radar control] on USS *Valley Forge* [CV-45] or USS *Boxer* [CV-21] to try to vector us [F9F Panthers of VF-51] to the B-36s. If that failed, we could always see a B-36 up there because the contrail was just humongous. If we didn't have a ship out at sea to vector us, we kept two airplanes on the flightline to go up and intercept a B-36.

'We had gun-camera film, and our chore was to intercept the B-36 and then fly in the wake with our gun cameras running, taking pictures all the time to show us battling with the wake and in the contrail. Then we would fly right by the B-36 and come down and land. That film would be flown non-stop to Washington and shown the next day by the admirals. They kept asking for more gun-camera film, so we just kept sending it over a period of weeks.

'[The B-36 pilots] would usually look up at us and wave as we'd go by. We would fly right underneath the No 4 engine. I usually favoured going up the starboard side, and I would usually fly in the wake of the No 3 engine and then slide over under the No 4 engine. Usually, you had so much more speed than them that we'd just pull up and do a chandelle and look down at them. We'd wave, they would wave back and we would then go about our business.'

A rumour that US Navy jets were actually trying to shoot down B-36s was current after several returned from flights with holes in their rudders that looked like 20 mm cannon hits. It was eventually found that globules of oil leaking from the inboard engines were congealing in icy high-altitude temperatures (*text continues on page 43*)

Maintenance for B-36s required elaborate access equipment, particularly for work on the 46 ft 9 in vertical tail. B-36B-15 44-92071 was converted into D-45 configuration and subsequently lost near El Paso, Texas, on 11 December 1953. The crew had not heeded a ground-control advisory of high ground in the area and it crashed onto the western side of the Franklin Mountains in poor weather when at an altitude of 5200 ft. Lt Col Herman F Gerick and his nine-man crew all perished (*USAF*)

COLOUR PLATES

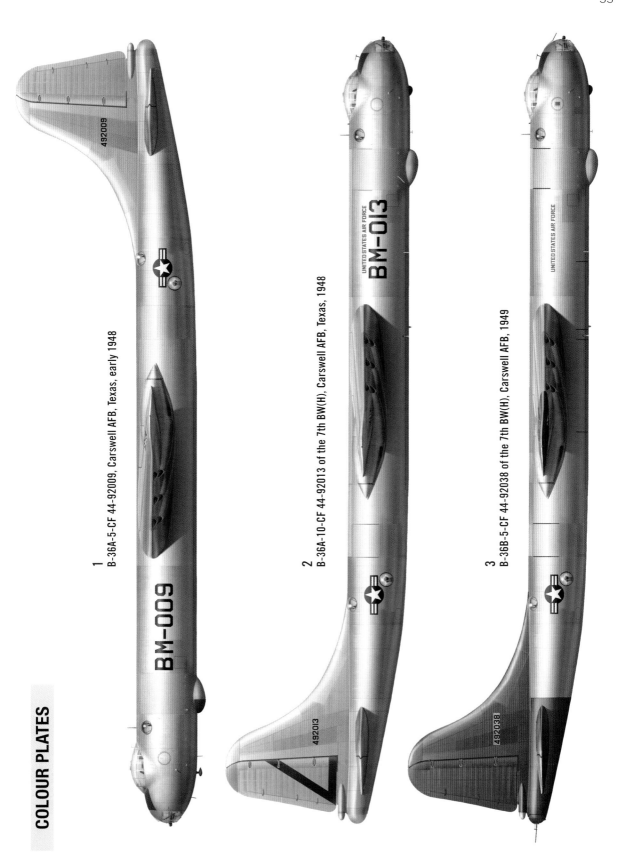

1
B-36A-5-CF 44-92009, Carswell AFB, Texas, early 1948

2
B-36A-10-CF 44-92013 of the 7th BW(H), Carswell AFB, Texas, 1948

3
B-36B-5-CF 44-92038 of the 7th BW(H), Carswell AFB, 1949

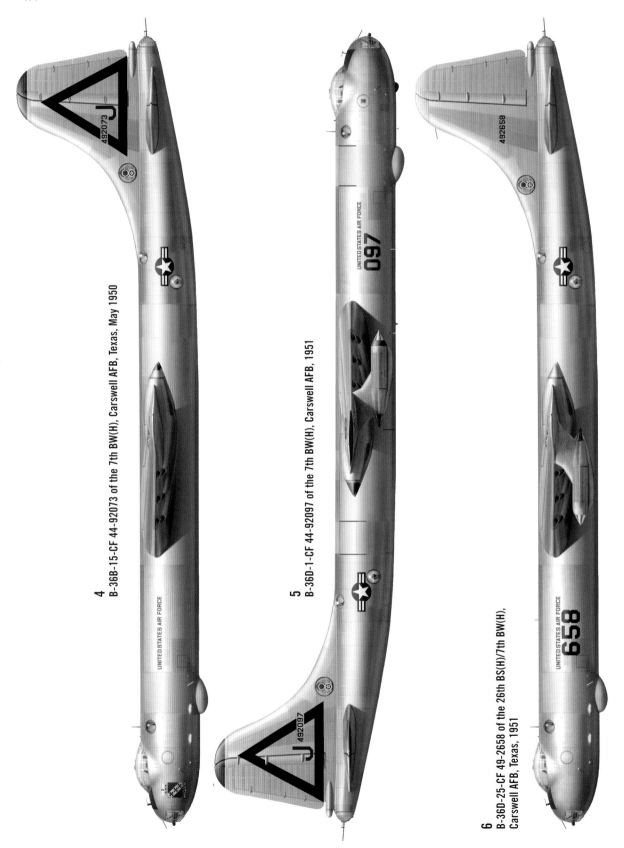

4
B-36B-15-CF 44-92073 of the 7th BW(H), Carswell AFB, Texas, May 1950

5
B-36D-1-CF 44-92097 of the 7th BW(H), Carswell AFB, 1951

6
B-36D-25-CF 49-2658 of the 26th BS(H)/7th BW(H),
Carswell AFB, Texas, 1951

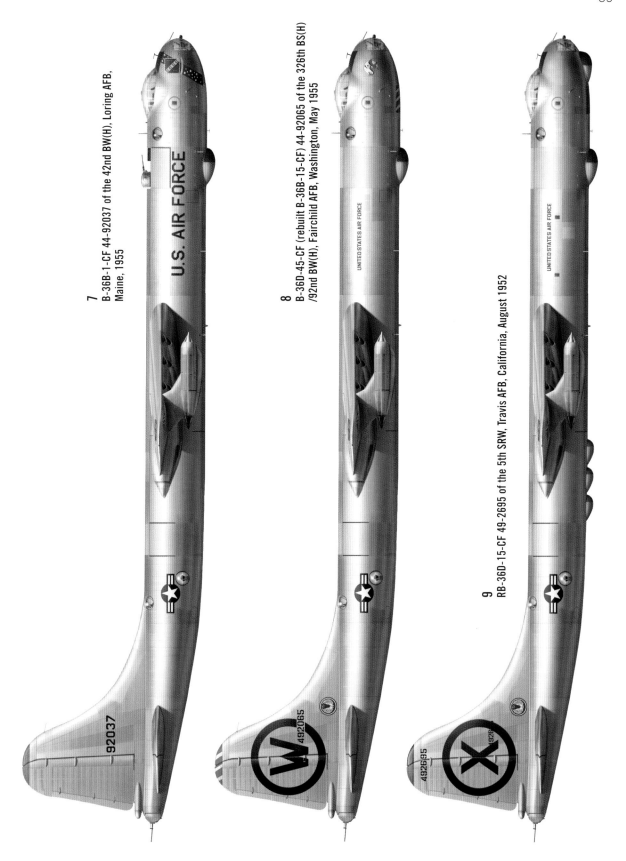

7
B-36B-1-CF 44-92037 of the 42nd BW(H), Loring AFB, Maine, 1955

8
B-36D-45-CF (rebuilt B-36B-15-CF) 44-92065 of the 326th BS(H) /92nd BW(H), Fairchild AFB, Washington, May 1955

9
RB-36D-15-CF 49-2695 of the 5th SRW, Travis AFB, California, August 1952

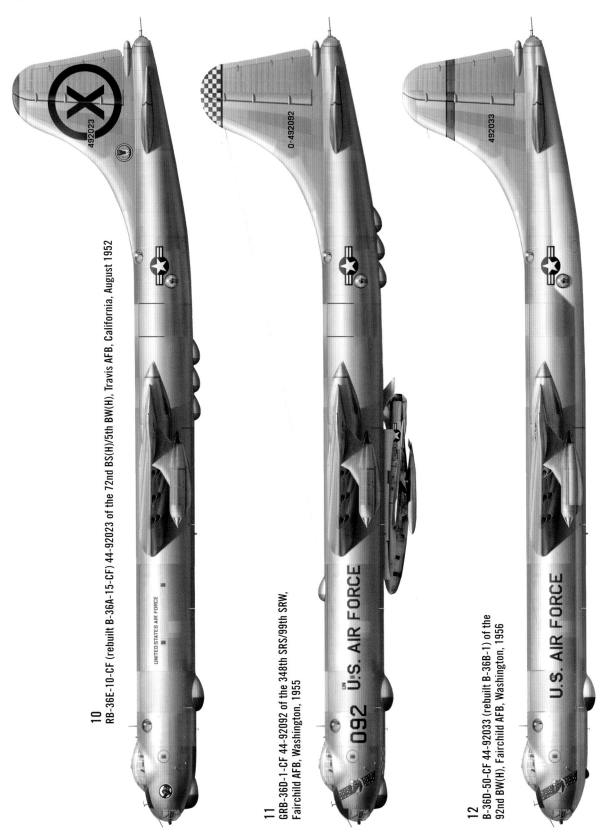

10
RB-36E-10-CF (rebuilt B-36A-15-CF) 44-92023 of the 72nd BS(H)/5th BW(H), Travis AFB, California, August 1952

11
GRB-36D-1-CF 44-92092 of the 348th SRS/99th SRW,
Fairchild AFB, Washington, 1955

12
B-36D-50-CF 44-92033 (rebuilt B-36B-1) of the
92nd BW(H), Fairchild AFB, Washington, 1956

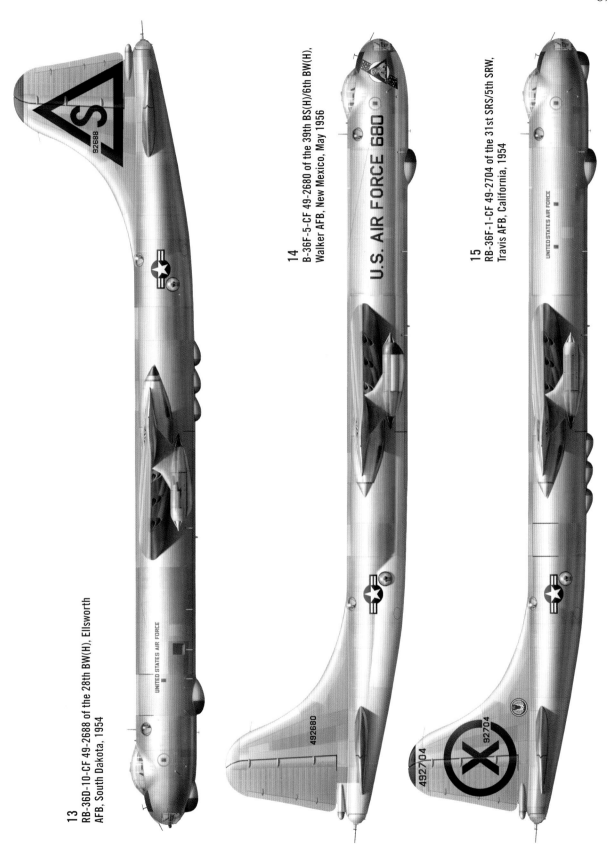

13
RB-36D-10-CF 49-2688 of the 28th BW(H), Ellsworth AFB, South Dakota, 1954

14
B-36F-5-CF 49-2680 of the 39th BS(H)/6th BW(H), Walker AFB, New Mexico, May 1956

15
RB-36F-1-CF 49-2704 of the 31st SRS/5th SRW, Travis AFB, California, 1954

92688

U.S. AIR FORCE 680

UNITED STATES AIR FORCE

492680

492704

92704

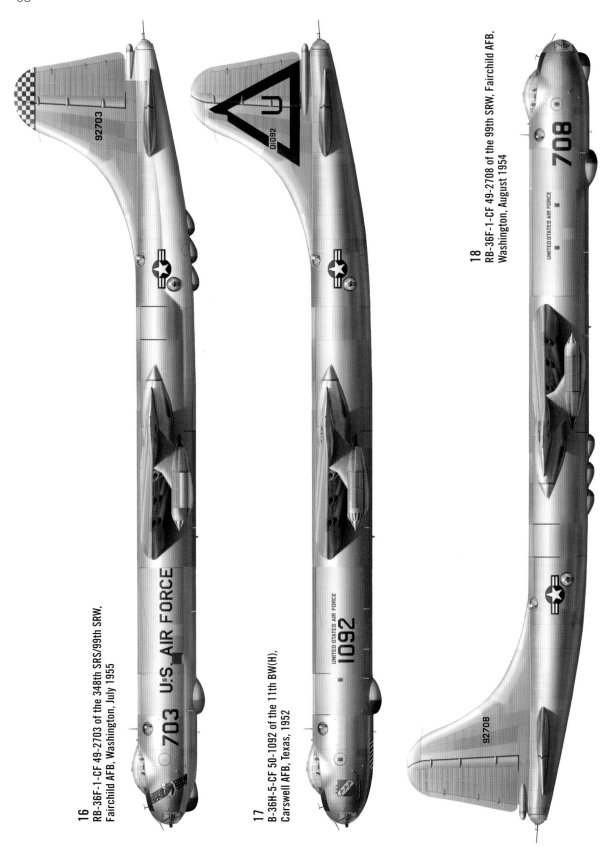

16
RB-36F-1-CF 49-2703 of the 348th SRS/99th SRW,
Fairchild AFB, Washington, July 1955

17
B-36H-5-CF 50-1092 of the 11th BW(H),
Carswell AFB, Texas, 1952

18
RB-36F-1-CF 49-2708 of the 99th SRW, Fairchild AFB,
Washington, August 1954

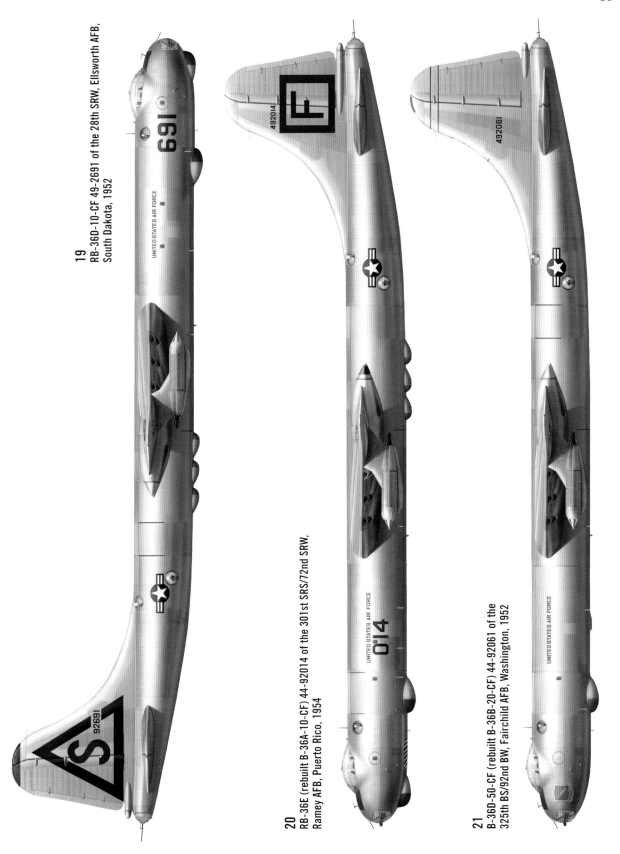

19
RB-36D-10-CF 49-2691 of the 28th SRW, Ellsworth AFB, South Dakota, 1952

20
RB-36E (rebuilt B-36A-10-CF) 44-92014 of the 301st SRS/72nd SRW, Ramey AFB, Puerto Rico, 1954

21
B-36D-50-CF (rebuilt B-36B-20-CF) 44-92061 of the 325th BS/92nd BW, Fairchild AFB, Washington, 1952

22
B-36H-10-CF 51-5704 of the 7th BW, Carswell AFB,
Texas, 1958

23
B-36H-1-CF 50-1086 of the 7th BW, Eglin AFB, Florida,
October 1955

24
JB-36H-55-CF 52-1358 of the 4925th Test Group
(Atomic), Kirtland AFB, New Mexico, 1957

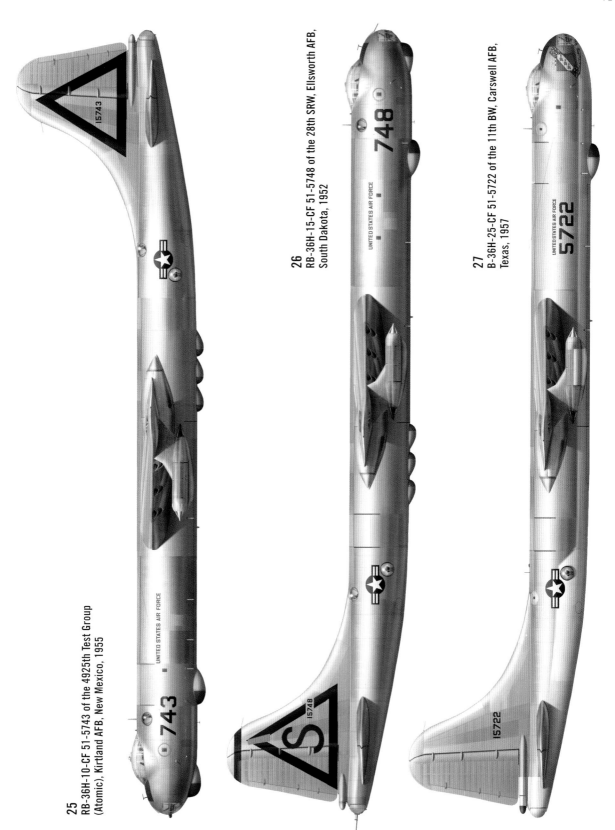

25
RB-36H-10-CF 51-5743 of the 4925th Test Group
(Atomic), Kirtland AFB, New Mexico, 1955

26
RB-36H-15-CF 51-5748 of the 28th SRW, Ellsworth AFB,
South Dakota, 1952

27
B-36H-25-CF 51-5722 of the 11th BW, Carswell AFB,
Texas, 1957

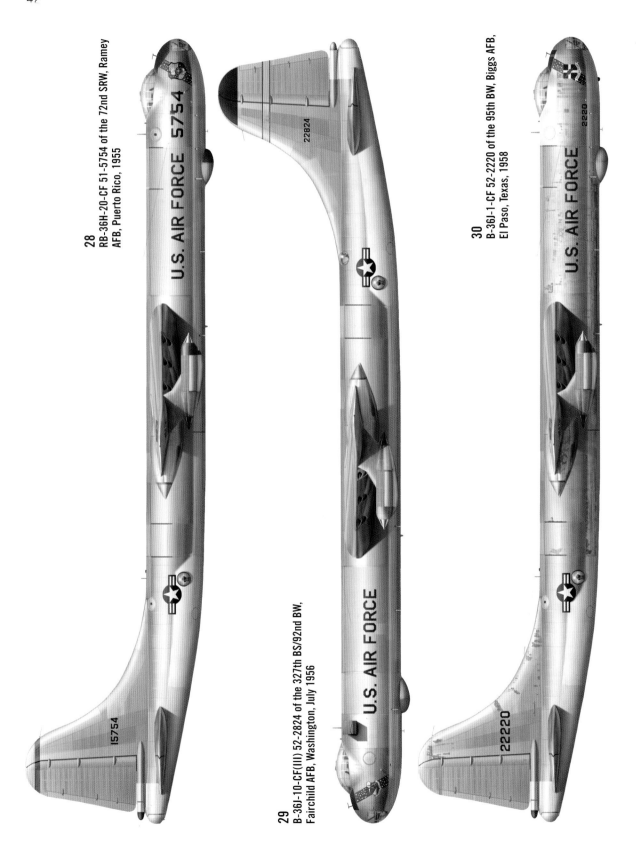

28
RB-36H-20-CF 51-5754 of the 72nd SRW, Ramey AFB, Puerto Rico, 1955

29
B-36J-10-CF(III) 52-2824 of the 327th BS/92nd BW, Fairchild AFB, Washington, July 1956

30
B-36J-1-CF 52-2220 of the 95th BW, Biggs AFB, El Paso, Texas, 1958

and penetrating the skin of the rudder. Because the oil then liquified at lower altitudes and ran down inside the rudder, the phenomenon was not discovered until cameras were fitted to a B-36.

Rudders were often vulnerable components on B-36s, particularly in strong crosswinds or when subjected to heavy manoeuvring. 99th SRW RB-36F-1-CF 49-2703 lost its rudder en route to making a ceremonial flypast at the Air Force Academy. It completed the flight safely. Other B-36s were able to land with missing rudders.

By October 1949 US Navy F3D Skyknights had made successful night radar interceptions of B-36s at 40,000 ft. Naval fighters tended to have lower wing loading than contemporary USAF interceptors, giving them better high-altitude manoeuvrability. Air Defence Command's F-89 Scorpions had particular difficulty in reaching the altitude of 99th SRW B-36s during practice interceptions over Michigan in December 1956.

However, the bomber's potential vulnerability to fighters was never tested. It was not used in the Korean War, officially because there were no targets that required such heavy bombing, although several high-altitude bomb damage assessment and target photographic missions were flown over Manchuria by 91st Strategic Reconnaissance Squadron (SRS) RB-36Ds from Yokota AB, Japan, in 1952. Within a few years the rapid progress in Soviet fighter development would limit the B-36's superiority in altitude over enemy territory.

PARALLEL PLANS

Convair's funding allowed for B-36 production until July 1948, although it was more realistically extended until November 1949 at the rate of four aircraft per month. Funding to cover the seven-month extension was needed, and this required the approval of the newly formed Aircraft and Weapons Board. A complication and possible further delay arose over the proposed replacement of the B-36A's engines with Variable Discharge Turbines (VDT) in a B-36C variant within the same production schedule.

VDT was an attempt to increase the aircraft's range to the original 10,000-mile requirement while also improving its speed to 410 mph and altitude to 45,000 ft. It involved a new version of the R-4360 engine developing 4360 hp which was already scheduled for the B-50. For the B-36, major changes would be required as the tractor propellers had to operate in six slender ten-foot-long nacelles on the leading edge of the wing, driven by long shafts extending from the engines to the rear of the wing.

New cooling ducts were needed in the leading edges and jet thrust would be created by new General Electric CHM-2 turbosuperchargers with variable discharge nozzles which replaced the existing internal superchargers. All of the engine's hot exhaust gases were discharged through a turbosupercharger (or turbine) to turn its blades, rather than being wasted at medium altitudes. The turbine functioned as a jet engine but without the usual burner cans, relying instead on the heat of the exhaust gases created by being 'burned' inside the engine's piston chambers. A two-stage centrifugal compressor supercharged all the intake air for the main engine and fed the compressed air into the engine's cylinders.

This evolutionary step towards a pure turboprop design, known as a compound engine, allowed the engine to run more efficiently due to better cooling of the air passing into the engine by an aftercooler. The turbine added around 300 hp and its variable nozzle was used to control the engine's power output. Although the R-4360-VDT was tested with some success in a B-50C, the complications in trying to install it in the proposed B-36C version with adequate cooling proved insurmountable and the engine would actually have been less powerful than the standard R-4360-41. VDT was cancelled before being installed in a B-36 prototype, as was the proposal to convert 34 production B-36s into C-models.

At the same time Gen Joseph McNarney, head of the USAF's Air Materiel Command, outlined four proposals for the B-36 in light of the B-36C cancellation, three of which recommended early termination of the programme. In one scenario only 22 would have been built. Gen Lauris Norstad, Deputy Air Force Chief of Staff, wanted only 66 aircraft, some of them converted to aerial tankers.

Consolidated fought back against those who were still pushing for cancellation or reduction of the B-36 plans by sending test pilot Erickson and a B-36A on a series of long-distance demonstration flights. One took B-36A 44-92013 on a journey of 33 hrs 10 min, flying repeatedly between Fort Worth and San Diego and delivering a 10,000-lb bomb load on a range during the 6992-mile excursion. Erickson and Witchell made another 33-hour round trip to Hawaii in May 1948, covering 8062 miles. Although the B-36's enemies still emphasised its relatively slow speeds on these trips, no other bomber could achieve that intercontinental range at the time.

After a series of presentations in Washington, DC and more fears of final cancellation of the project during the subsequent discussions, Secretary of the Air Force Stuart Symington, Gen Kenney (who had favoured the B-50 instead), Gen Norstad and other opponents agreed to fund 95 B-36A/Bs. It is likely that their objections may have been tempered by witnessing some spectacular flying by Erickson and Witchell that showed off the bomber's speed and agility, including a steep take-off followed by a pass at an altitude of about 30 ft.

The revelation of active Soviet hostility to the West in the blockade of the Western Zone of Berlin, necessitating the Berlin Airlift, focused minds on the scarcity of US forces in Europe and the USAF's reliance on the ageing B-29 as its only available strategic bomber in any more severe crisis. Production of at least 61 B-36s was agreed on 24 May 1948, coinciding with the start of the massive Berlin airlift operation.

Despite this evidence for its potential value, the 'Peacemaker's' enemies elsewhere were not silenced. As part of its burgeoning war with the other US services over the allocation of defence funds, the US Navy began to circulate reports of the B-36A's teething troubles, including persistent propeller vibration and engine cooling inadequacies, fuel tank leaks and electrical systems faults. The Admirals' opposition gathered momentum in 1949 and continued until 1951, when the massive increase in defence spending caused by the Korean War boosted all three services, and eventually included funds for the first of a different type of supercarrier, the Forrestal class.

CHAPTER FOUR

SERVICE ENTRY

Victim of two separate engine fire incidents during its short service career, B-36B-1 44-92035 of the 26th BS/7th BW was written off on 22 November 1950 after a series of inflight failures with its R-4360s, electrical faults and fires, with the loss of two crew. Seen here in a Project GEM Arctic red paint scheme, the bomber was photographed in formation with a TB-25 Mitchell crew trainer (*USAF*)

The USAAF's Air Training Command established a B-36 Mobile Training Unit at Carswell AFB in early 1947, and in its first year 1500 personnel completed the course to tackle the bomber's considerable technical challenges. All maintenance work was carried out in the open, facing the extremes of baking Texan summer heat and winter chill as there were no hangars large enough to house a B-36. An engine assembly line was established at the base to add external components to the basic core engines delivered from Pratt & Whitney.

One of the longest maintenance jobs was changing the numerous spark plugs (partly caused by the high lead content in the fuel), but this wasted time and was later reduced by using longer-lasting, platinum-tipped plugs. Alternators were also very unreliable in early B-36s, sometimes leaving aircraft in danger of suffering a total loss of electrical power. In flight, the engineer could work his way along the catwalk inside the wing to access each engine's electrical panel if circuit breakers needed re-setting.

For all crew members, the constant, jarring low-frequency vibration from the six mighty engines was the loud and intrusive background to their work and a source of exhaustion in itself. Communication with crewmen in adjacent positions was often done with hand signals.

Generating the necessary aircrews was an equally massive task amidst post-war austerity. The USAF's officer numbers had been reduced, and many positions, including navigator and bombardier slots, were filled by enlisted master sergeants or technical sergeants in 1949.

The B-36A's continuing bugs, most of which had been correctly identified in an unwelcome critique by the US Navy, took some time to be worked out. Bomb-bay doors iced up and stuck at altitude, fuel and oil leaks still occurred and engine cooling fans could not cope with the high operating temperatures. Some individual propellers' tendency to put themselves in reverse at low speeds, causing a sudden yaw to one side on landing, required revision of the relevant circuit breakers. However, the B-36As only remained in service very briefly, most having been converted into RB-36E reconnaissance bombers by July 1951.

The B-36B soon followed, having flown on 8 July 1948 (only two weeks after delivery of the 7th BG's first B-36A), but its service life would also be very brief as most B-models had been converted into B-36Ds by February 1952. Its more powerful 3500 hp R-4360-41 engines with water injection significantly boosted performance. B-36Bs could reach 42,500 ft and 381 mph.

In a record-breaking flight from Carswell AFB on 29 January 1949, B-36B 44-92043 dropped two 42,000-lb dummy bombs on Muroc (later, Edwards AFB) bomb range, one of them from 40,000 ft. Although the drop emphasised some centre of gravity pitch-up concerns when such heavy bombs were carried in tandem in separate bays, it also highlighted the B-36's capability as a heavy, high-altitude bomber. Nothing else in the inventory offered such capability, and even its survivability in combat was now defended by its previous critics. Gen Kenney commented, 'How are you going to shoot down a bomber at night flying at 40,000 ft with a solid overcast?' In ongoing tests, a lightly loaded 7th BW B-36 had reached 50,000 ft, far above the XB-36's projected maximum ceiling.

The B-36B introduced the K-1 bombing/navigation system, a combination of radar, altimeter, compass and bombing equipment that had been in development since 1944. It was originally designated AN/APQ-23, with an AN/APQ-13 search radar linked to a Norden M-9 bombsight – a combination that worked quite effectively at an altitude of 30,000 ft and a speed of 400 mph in B-29 and B-50 bombers. The system evolved for the B-36A used the AN/APS-23 search radar and Sperry SRC-1 (later, A-1) computer.

Sperry also worked on an optical, vertical periscopic bombsight, a design that was later passed to the Farrand Optical Company and was designated Y-1. This system developed into the AN/APQ-24 for the B-36B, and it proved to be extremely accurate (despite potential interference from the defensive armament electronics) if full calibration was conducted before a flight. One advantage of the AN/APQ-24 system was that it allowed the bombardier to take evasive action during a bombing run. From 30,000 ft the radar could scan an area 75 miles in radius, including large city targets, at distances of up to 200 miles or shipping at 50 to 100 miles. The dated but still reliable World War 2-era Norden bombsight was retained as a back-up.

In April 1948 the AN/APS-23 radar and Sperry A-1 electro-mechanical bombing computer became the K-1 system, and it was tested in a B-29 and in B-36B 44-92072 the following month. The complex 1500-lb system demonstrated a tracking range of more than 28 miles, and it could be used in faster aircraft at speeds up to 800 mph. Employing a combination of optical 'fixes' (by the navigator and observers) and radar sighting, the system computed and supplied data either to the autopilot or directly to the pilot, while also exactly measuring the bomber's position. It could release bombs automatically too, leaving the K-system crew member with the task of entering data for wind correction and bomb ballistics into the computer and focusing the sight on the target, or on a suitable known offset point if the target was not clearly visible.

The first K-1-equipped B-36B was delivered in February 1950, and the system also appeared in B-36Ds from August of that year. Once in service, the B-model's AN/APQ-24 suffered from poor reliability and availability rates of around 25 per cent, compared with 70 per cent for the previous AN/APQ-23. This was attributed to inadequate technical crew training, as earlier tests had shown it to be extremely reliable, although it was susceptible to jamming. There were also reservations about the definition of the imagery on the radar scope. Throughout 1951 the system's dependability improved, and the upgraded K-3A was fitted to B-36s. It had an improved computer, the Sperry A-1A, and a better Y-3 periscope sight. It became the standard system for B-36s from the D-model onwards.

The 73 B-36Bs also had the full complement of 16 defensive guns and an AN/APG-3 gun-laying radar for the tail weapons, although its vacuum tube-powered radar often proved to be unreliable. The radar was intended to track and lock on to a single target. AN/APG-32A twin-radome versions were installed in later B-36Fs. A final version, the AN/APG-41 for later B-36H/Js, used a single, wider radome.

The upper turrets extended and folded outwards within seconds of their cover panels being retracted. The lower fuselage turrets dropped downwards, folding outwards to extend the guns. Firing the guns transmitted noise and vibration throughout the aircraft interior. Installation of the heavy guns could in itself be a hazardous process, as they had to be carried up maintenance stands close to the wings and then along the top of the fuselage to their respective turrets – an unenviable task in icy conditions.

Loading the ammunition aboard was one of the main tasks before each flight, and it was considered a dirty and arduous job. The ammunition belts, each up to eight feet long, were carried onto the fuselage surface for the four upper turrets and carefully passed down to gunners. Rounds had to be correctly aligned in their feed trays to avoid jams. Ammunition for the tail turret was fed through an access slot in the rear fuselage. Usually, the ammunition was completely fired out during a mission to test the system. If guns had

Re-arming the nose turret required deft footwork and strength to haul heavy belts of 20 mm ammunition into place, with access panels having first been removed from the area. The hemispheric gunsight is visible to the left of the central circular section of the 'greenhouse', with its AN/APS-54 radar warning receiver (*USAF*)

been required in action, the radar would have been the only means of sighting them for Gen LeMay forbade the use of tracer ammunition in SAC aircraft.

As production methods became more efficient new B-36Bs were rolling out of Plant 4 more frequently by December 1948. Routine B-model training flights included a climb to 10,000 ft, where the weapons would be armed. A cruise at 10,000 ft at speeds best suited to the intended range was followed by a climb to 25,000 ft within 30 minutes of the target. After the bomb run at higher ('normal') speed, the crew then flew an evasive course for 15 minutes and a ten-minute escape route. They then returned to long-range cruise speed and altitude and disarmed the weapons before returning to base.

In the early 1950s, LeMay kept his crews at high alert, flying frequent simulated nuclear attacks on unsuspecting American cities and maintaining 24-hour combat readiness. He later claimed that 'San Francisco has been bombed more than 600 times in a month'.

Brig Gen 'Bill' Irvine, who took command of the 7th BW from 3 January 1950, ordered that all training missions should last for 24 hours, setting off at 1000 hrs and returning at the same time the next day. Failure to keep to this schedule became a serious disciplinary offence. Irvine, expert in aircraft engineering, had been ordered by LeMay to improve overall efficiency and sort out the persistent maintenance and mechanical problems that still kept so many B-36s grounded.

He also helped to make sense of the supply of spare parts. The administration system required Carswell to order parts from the central San Antonio centre at Kelly AFB, almost 400 miles away, after they had been delivered there from Fort Worth – just a few minutes from Carswell. Long delays resulted while the parts were flown back to the latter site. Brig Gen Irvine short-circuited that process by having parts delivered directly from Consolidated Vultee a few hundred yards from his Carswell maintenance areas.

PROMOTING THE BEHEMOTH

Carswell soon became a popular port of call for politicians and celebrities keen to be seen with the world's most impressive bomber and book a 'joy ride' in it. At a time when fear of communist aggression was a major public concern, the B-36 units provided powerful imagery of the SAC deterrent to reassure Americans.

Consolidated Vultee produced 'Target-Peace', a B-36 documentary in 1949 that featured flypasts by 11 B-36As, showing B-36Bs on the production line and glimpses of the B-36D and its XC-99 transport version against a strongly patriotic soundtrack. RKO Pictures used an early B-36D (49-2652 with fake 'triangle L' tail markings) as the 'star' of its production *High Frontier*, employing the expertise of 436th BS commander Lt Col John Bartlett. A B-36 cockpit was mocked up and air-to-air footage was shot at Carswell, but studio owner Howard Hughes lost interest in the film project and it was never completed.

Brief B-36 appearances were included in other films featuring nuclear war scenarios, and the collaborative effort by Gen LeMay, actor James

Stewart and screenwriter Lt Col Beirne Lay Jr resulted in the most memorable B-36 film of them all, *Strategic Air Command*. Lay, a World War 2 B-24 bomb group commander whose autobiographical novel had been turned into the film *Twelve O'Clock High*, was close to LeMay. He wrote the screenplay for *High Frontier* and engaged the interest of LeMay and Oscar-winning actor James Stewart for the new film, extending the ideas of *High Frontier* for a wider audience in VistaVision. In November 1943 Stewart had commanded the 703rd BS, an Eighth Air Force B-24 unit, and by 1945 he was in charge of the 2nd Bomb Wing. Post-war, he retained a reserve USAAF commission.

Filming by Paramount Pictures began at Carswell on 4 February 1954 with a large production crew. B-36H 51-5734 (with a couple of similarly marked substitutes), flown mainly by Lt Col George N Payne, was used for the impressive aerial sequences. The plot, featuring a B-36 that catches fire during cold-weather tests over Greenland and crash-lands on snowy terrain after the crew had bailed out, had echoes of earlier real B-36 losses. Stewart continued to fly into the 1960s, completing a B-52 mission over North Vietnam and hitting Mach 2 in a Convair B-58A Hustler. Beirne Lay received an Academy Award nomination in the Best Motion Picture Story category in 1955 for *Strategic Air Command*.

LeMay kept up his B-36-boosting campaign with overflights of the Air Force Association's July 1949 National Convention in Chicago. Each day seven B-36s flew over the city in formation. In 1948–49, LeMay sent B-36 overflight demonstrations to 13 high-profile public events ranging from the Cleveland Air Races to a sonorous cruise over Washington, DC to impress Congress and officially celebrate 45 years since the Wright brothers' first flight in a far less substantial craft. The public soon became well acquainted with their costly new protector. Five B-36A/Bs from the 7th BW overflew the Capitol Building to mark the inauguration of President Harry S Truman on 20 January 1949. He restricted the defence budget in that year, but the B-36 survived while other USAF aircraft purchases were cut.

MISHAPS

Aircraft accidents were far from uncommon in the 1950s, and when they occurred to such a wide-winged warrior as the B-36 they inevitably received disproportionate media attention, despite intense SAC security. Safety statistics for the bomber were actually above average, allowing for its prolonged flights in difficult conditions. In SAC service some units had unusually good safety records. The 72nd SRW, flying RB-36s from October 1952 to January 1959 from Ramey AFB, Puerto Rico, had only one ground accident during that time, and the 99th SRW at Fairchild AFB, in Washington, had no major mishaps at all during its five years with the aircraft from 1951 to 1956.

However, the B-36's complexity and persistent technical problems led to 32 crashes. The first happened at Carswell AFB on 15 September 1949 after three years of accident-free flying when 9th BS/7th BW B-36B 44-92079, flown by Maj Roy Husband, crashed during a night maximum-effort exercise. Two of its propellers inexplicably went into reverse during the take-off run and the aircraft rose briefly to ten feet, before running off the end of the runway into Lake Worth, where it sank. Five crew perished.

At the time there was no way to detect whether a propeller had reversed its pitch, and after another B-36 had two propellers suddenly reverse while landing, a visual check was instigated prior to the bomber taxiing out. A crew member had to stand in front of the aircraft and check all propellers in the 'LeMay Shuffle' or 'Vandenberg Shuffle' (Gen Hoyt Vandenberg was the USAF Chief of Staff) as the engines were run up for take-off. Suitable propeller reverse indicator lights were installed in later B-36s.

Multiple malfunctions brought down the 7th BW's B-36B 44-92035 on 22 November 1950. This 492nd BS aircraft, which had completed a record 9600-mile flight around the USA in 43 hrs 37 min on 12 March 1949 with a ten-man crew commanded by Capt Roy Showalter, initially suffered an engine fire minutes after take-off. Another blaze in the AN/APQ-24 radar caused by vibration from gun-firing later in the mission was followed by electrical failure of two of the gun turrets and a second engine malfunction.

With only one functioning engine on the left wing, the pilot headed for Kelly AFB, Texas, only to discover that gun-firing vibration had also knocked out the electrical circuits controlling the engines. When bad weather prevented the aircraft from recovering at two diversion bases, its crew had to head back to Carswell. When another engine failed, the crew bailed out near Cleburne, Texas. One died when his parachute failed to open and a second was killed when his head collided with a static inboard propeller blade. For the forward compartment crew to bail out of the round hatch in the fuselage side, the No 3 propeller had to be feathered. They then performed a 'stand and roll' escape movement to clear the airframe on exit. Normal crew entry to the bomber was via a ladder in the nose-wheel bay.

In a previous engine fire incident on 19 July 1949, 44-92035 literally lost an engine at 40,000 ft when it burned through its mountings and fell off the wing, justifying the decision to mount the R-4360-41s on the wings' trailing edges. Pilot Capt Harold Barry, who would later be involved in the first 'Broken Arrow' (lost nuclear weapon) incident, then found that the other two engines on the same wing had stopped due to circuit failure with the electrical controls. He managed to return the bomber safely to Carswell on that occasion with only three engines.

Clearly, the B-36 still had many technical challenges to overcome before it could be declared truly operational. The R-4360-41 engines were

Heading back to Ellsworth AFB, RB-36H-25 51-13720 of the 28th SRW lost power on take-off from Lowry AFB, Colorado, on 15 November 1956 due to frozen fuel lines. Its pilot, Capt Regis Powers, climbed to 1500 ft and attempted a recovery at nearby Stapleton Airport in Denver, Colorado, but the bomber crashed in a field a mile short of the runway. Braving fierce magnesium fires and exploding ammunition, rescuers got all 21 crew out alive, including one who was trapped in the severed nose section for an hour (*USAF*)

a constant source of concern. Fires broke out through carburettor faults or leaking exhausts and their propeller governors, alternators, cooling systems and ignition circuits gave engineers frequent crises to handle. It was considered almost normal to have a B-36B return from a flight with at least one engine out of action. Remedies were introduced, and eventually engines more routinely reached their 300-hour limits prior to replacement without serious faults.

Biggs AFB, near El Paso, Texas, was the home of the 95th BW – the tenth B-36 wing to be established when its three squadrons converted to B-36Ds in November 1952, although crews used RB-36Fs for much of their training programme. Biggs also housed the 97th BW, which was transitioning to the B-47. The arrival of the Boeing bomber meant that the runway needed extending to 13,500 ft. It was also widened by 300 ft in order to accommodate the B-36.

Standard 24-hour missions soon became routine, with the pre-flight process commencing a full 24 hours before take-off. The latter included a complete walk-around inspection, with a second walk-around and internal inspection being performed four hours before take-off. Despite this rigorous routine, it was unusual to return to base with all six engines still operating. Although it was often possible to compensate for loss of power at altitude, sudden engine failure on final landing approach with the landing gear down was a deadly situation. On 28 August 1954 Maj Lanier's B-36D 44-92097 (of the 7th BW) lost three engines on one side in that situation and he had to crash-land in the desert, having narrowly missed a motel building in El Paso. The aircraft burned out but only one crewman, Ron Strasheim, was lost.

Accidents could be caused by the B-36's sheer size and weight when moving on the ground. 42nd BW B-36D 49-2664 had propeller problems on a flight from Carswell on 5 June 1953 and it returned to base. While taxiing back to the dispersal, the brakes failed due to a broken hydraulic line and the pilot was unable to stop his aircraft from running into a 7th BW B-36H, causing severe damage to both bombers.

RB-36E 44-92022 was involved in a similar mishap at Travis AFB (named Fairfield-Suisun until 1951), in California, after returning in darkness from a 15-hour flight. While taxiing into its parking area the brakes failed and the aircraft ran into RB-36E 44-92019. Although there were no crew injuries, and 44-92022 suffered only minor damage, the collision destroyed most of 44-92019's forward fuselage ahead of the turret bay. The whole of its nose area had to be replaced by a newly manufactured unit, grafted on at Travis AFB in April 1951 in Operation 'Pinocchio'.

The approximately 30,000-gallon fuel load of a B-36 was in itself a major hazard during its service life. B-36F 49-2679 of the 7th BW was being refuelled at Carswell AFB on 4 August 1952 when fuel overflowed from its No 3 tank vent. Heavy rainfall carried the fuel under a B-10 ground power start cart, where hot exhaust ignited it. The fire leapt up the stream of leaking fuel and entered the aircraft's fuel tanks, causing a major fire that quickly incinerated the bomber. Groundcrew rapidly towed other nearby B-36s to safety. Another 7th BW aircraft, B-36F 50-1067, burned out when leaking fuel ignited after it had a landing gear collapse on touch-down at Carswell AFB.

TARZON AND 'FAT MAN'

It was perhaps inevitable that many new types of weapon were suggested to take advantage of the B-36's gigantic carrying capacity. The earliest remote-controlled, radio-guided bombs were tested towards the end of World War 2, including Bell Aircraft's VB-13 Tarzon. Based on the British, Barnes Wallis-designed 12,000-lb Tallboy 'earthquake bomb' dropped by RAF Lancasters on German submarine pens, V-weapon sites and the battleship *Tirpitz*, it was given four ailerons and rudder and elevator controls. Guided by an observer with a small joystick control visually following a flare attached to the bomb's tail, it was only a clear weather weapon. During the Korean War B-29s dropped 30 Tarzons, with a 25 per cent success rate against bridges and other hard targets.

Eighteen B-36Bs (44-92045 to 44-92062) were adapted to carry Tarzon, these aircraft being fitted with an updated guidance system that featured a radio link and a television screen for the controller to watch the missile's progress via a camera in its nose. The 92nd BW deployed Tarzon-equipped B-36s to Japan, Okinawa and Guam in August 1953 as the war ground to its conclusion, and they were not required to test these weapons in action.

The aircraft's striking power had been amply demonstrated five years earlier on 7–8 December 1948 – the seventh anniversary of the Pearl Harbor attack – when a 7th BG B-36B flown by Maj John D ('Big John') Bartlett flew non-stop from Carswell to Honolulu, Hawaii, via an overflight of San Diego. It carried a crew of 15 and an inert 10,000-lb bomb, which it dropped before arriving over Pearl Harbor. The 8100-mile round trip, arranged by Gen LeMay, took 35 hours to complete.

Embarrassingly, the huge bomber penetrated Hawaiian airspace without being detected on radar. Forces defending Hawaii complained that they had not been forewarned of the flight, and the mission was tactfully classified as 'Restricted' in official documents.

Bartlett returned to Hawaii in June 1950, this time landing his B-36 at Hickam AFB during a 10,000-mile demonstration flight across the Pacific. The rest of the B-36s involved in the exercise took different routes to overfly Kwajalein, in the Marshall Islands, before rendezvousing near Hawaii and then completing their 10,000-mile journeys.

Even more impressive, and also good publicity for SAC's new 'big stick', was the 9600-mile flight in March 1949, again with Maj Bartlett as pilot. He flew from Fort Worth to Minneapolis, Minnesota, and Great Falls, Montana, then on to Key West, Florida, before returning to Great Falls and then recovering to Fort Worth via Spokane, Washington. The record journey of 45 hrs 37 min, with enough fuel left for another two hours of flight time, convinced Bartlett that they could have met SAC's original 10,000-mile range target. For almost half its time aloft the aircraft had a 10,000-lb bomb load on board. These flights were well publicised, allowing any potential enemy to easily calculate how much of their territory was at risk from B-36s operating from bases in the extreme north of America, or Japan or the Azores.

Training missions soon consisted of 24-hour flights, and the longest of all B-36 missions was made on 14–16 January 1951 when Convair personnel took RB-36D 44-92090 on an endurance marathon lasting all of 51 hours. For many crews, earning the coveted 'Convair 1000 hours' pin took a surprisingly short time.

Throughout this period of early range-testing flights, the force size at Carswell AFB continued to grow. The 7th BW had initially controlled just the 7th BG, but on 1 December 1948 the 11th BG (Heavy), which had previously flown B-29s from Guam, was also established at Carswell. Its initial personnel came from the 7th BG, and it was eventually activated on 16 February 1951 with Brig Gen Thomas Gerrity in command.

SAC had originally planned for 18 B-36s to be operated by three squadrons of six bombers in each group, but this number was increased to 30 aircraft per group in late 1948 with the addition of the 11th BG under Lt Col Harry Goldsworthy. A rather overcrowded Carswell then housed the 9th, 436th and 492nd BSs of the 7th BG, commanded by Col Alan D Clark, and the 26th, 42nd and 98th BSs of the 11th BG. As usual with a new type of aircraft, the initial crews had long experience, mainly on B-29s in Carswell's case.

JETS

The main criticism of the B-36B, as it achieved effective operational status, was its lack of speed – a shortcoming that became more significant as jet fighter performance steadily increased. Extra power from add-on jet engines was a low-cost compromise after the cancellation of VDT. Other proposals involving Wright T-35 or Northrop T-37 Turbodyne advanced turboprop engines were considered. As a quick solution, the proven General Electric J47 turbojet was favoured for installation in the B-36D, subsequent variants and the re-manufactured B-36A/Bs.

As a relatively lightweight engine developing 5200 lbs of thrust, the J47 could be mounted in podded pairs beneath each outer wing. The jets were intended for use on take-off to increase the potential combat load by up to 40,000 lbs and to boost dash speed over the target to 460 mph. When combined with the bomber's 40,000-ft altitude, rapid climb and fast run to the target area, such a speed would have complicated an intercepting fighter's job.

The jet pods for the J47 installation were similar to the B-47 Stratojet's, including the fitment of an identification light beneath the engines. The fairing aft of the light contained an outrigger undercarriage when used by the Boeing bomber, but it was empty when fitted to the B-36 (*USAF*)

For take-off, the jets were usually cranked up to 100 per cent power, allowing a loaded B-36 to get airborne well before the end of a SAC runway and climb away at 2000-3000 ft per minute. They could also be used together with an adjustment of the fuel mixture for the reciprocating engines to achieve rapid acceleration and a steep climb to high altitude in order to evade fighters.

The jet pods were slightly adapted from the versions manufactured for the inboard engines of the B-47. Their support struts and aerodynamic fairings were essentially the same and their taxi light installations were also retained. Each pod held a pair of J47-GE-19 turbojets, modified to burn the same aviation gasoline as the B-36's Wasp Major piston engines, albeit with a slight reduction in thrust. They had adjustable 'iris blade' aerodynamic covers that extended over the jet air intakes to reduce engine windmilling when the jets were not in use.

B-36B 44-92057 had the paired nacelles installed ready to start flight tests on 26 March 1949, although it retained the J35A-19 engines used in the B-47 as J47s were not available at the time. Installing them outboard on the B-36's very strong wings required little structural alteration or reinforcement. The extra weight of the pods on the outer wings did, however, slightly reduce lateral manoeuvrability, and the lack of powered flying controls became more noticeable.

Collapsible aerodynamic covers reduced drag when the engines were shut down, these being designed to allow a small amount of air to pass through and keep the compressor blades turning so that they did not freeze up. The jet engines were controlled in pairs, comprising one from each wing, so that the aircraft was not inadvertently destabilised (*Terry Panopalis Collection*)

With ten engines in operation ('four burning and six churning'), the not-infrequent loss of one or even two engines in flight was manageable. On rare occasions B-36s returned with all three reciprocating engines on one wing feathered, as long as the jets on that wing were running. When a crew informed an air base's air traffic control that they had a failed engine or two, they would be routinely asked if they wished to declare an emergency. The usual reply was, 'It's okay. We still have eight left'.

The J47s could also help to maintain stable flight if several 'recip' engines on one side failed. The engines' throttle systems operated on pairs of inboard and outboard jets to prevent asymmetric thrust, and consequent instability, occurring. The B-36's extraordinary 'engine out' survivability was demonstrated by Capt Barry H Young of the 7th BW on 10 December 1954. In an outstanding demonstration of piloting skill, he managed to land safely with all three piston engines on one wing feathered, no jet engines and no flaps.

CAMERAS

Gen LeMay insisted on very capable photo-reconnaissance versions of all his bombers as vital assets for obtaining accurate targeting information, day and night mapping and (in the B-36's case) post-strike imagery. As he pointed out to his crews in his usual peremptory way;

'We are all in the business, of course, to get bombs on the target and destroy targets. You can't destroy a target if you don't know where you are going and you don't know what to look for after you get there. I foresee in the future a reconnaissance outfit composed of people who are quite capable of not only carrying out the primary mission of reconnaissance but also capable of carrying out armed reconnaissance and putting bombs on targets as they are found.'

As the B-36 was the only bomber in existence capable of long-range delivery of nuclear weapons, reconnaissance data was even more vital. Around one-third of the B-36 production run were therefore built or converted into reconnaissance bomber versions. This programme was approved early in 1948, and it would result in similarly equipped reconnaissance version of the B-36D, E, F and H. An RB-36 version might deliver bombs and also conduct its own post-strike reconnaissance without risking separate photo-reconnaissance aircraft.

From the initial B-36 production it was decided in November 1948 that 21 B-36As and the sole YB-36 should be re-manufactured as RB-36Es. They re-appeared on the production line alongside the very similar new-build RB-36Ds. Remanufacturing them as RB-36Es required major structural work that meant stripping and disassembling their fuselages into main components, which were then mounted on specially built jigs for rework.

The entire fuselage section that had housed the forward bomb-bay had to be replaced to allow for a reconnaissance bay. Other basic modifications brought them up to B-36B standard, adding new pressure bulkheads for the camera bay and its crew. Radio intelligence-gathering equipment was installed, and they received underwing J47 jet pods, R-4360-41 engines, 20 mm defensive armament and other equipment updates to make them virtually the same as RB-36Ds.

With the further addition of magnesium-covered control surfaces instead of fabric and the later replacement of the cable-operated roller bomb-bay doors with two sets of more reliable quick-acting snap-open (or 'clam shell') versions, the modified B-36B 44-92057 essentially became the prototype B-52D. Flight tests showed that the jet pods caused vibration problems, which were cured by additional bracing struts.

With J35As installed, this flying testbed reached 400 mph and easily climbed to 40,000 ft, while the substitution of J47s was calculated to increase the speed over the target to an even safer 435 mph. In practice, 406 mph was a more realistic top speed figure, although the aircraft could now reach 43,800 ft. Combat weight was also significantly improved with the extra jet power, rising from the B-36B's typical 221,400 lbs to more than 251,900 lbs for an RB-36D.

The improvements in the RB-36D/E's suitability for the photo-reconnaissance role brought about a final decision to cancel the RB-49 on 12 December 1949, just as the B-36 was approaching the end of its original 100-aircraft contract. The last four examples were completed as B-36Ds, and seven RB-36Ds (originally scheduled as B-36Bs) had already been delivered from 3 June 1950 before any B-36Ds were completed. A second contract was issued in April 1949 for 22 B-36D bombers and 24 more RB-36Ds with similar performance characteristics to the B-36D, to be completed by June 1951.

In addition, 59 B-36Ds were converted from B-models by installing jet pods and quick-action bomb-bay doors at Convair's San Diego facility, as there was insufficient space to undertake this upgrade at Fort Worth. Conversion involved major structural work, including the removal of wings, control surfaces and bomb-bay doors. The first D-model, 44-92043, was completed by November 1951. The last of 57 brand new B/RB-36Ds was handed over in August 1951 and the final modified B/RB-36D in February 1952.

For the RB-36D (which first flew on 14 December 1949 and entered service several months ahead of the B-36D), the crew was increased by seven men to 22. Included amongst the latter was a photo technician, who had his own small darkroom in the pressurised 18-ft-long bay forward of the No 1 bomb-bay in which to re-load film cartridges for up to 17 advanced cameras also installed there. There were no film processing facilities, however. The cameras included K-17C, K-22A, K-38 and K-40 models, photographing through windows in the belly of the compartment – each window was covered by a sliding external door. Bomb-bay doors were eliminated for the forward bay, and its magnesium skin was replaced by aluminium to tolerate the pressurisation in the compartment.

RB-36D-10 49-2688 on a pre-delivery flight from Fort Worth in September 1950 with shiny new aluminium and duller magnesium panels. The three 'ferret' ECM radomes beneath the No 4 bomb-bay were later moved aft to allow carriage of large nuclear weapons (*Author's Collection*)

Although the RB-36D/Es were not initially intended to carry bombs, and the K-3 bombing system was duly removed, the No 2 bomb-bay could take 80 100-lb T86 flash bombs for night reconnaissance. The third bay could also carry flash bombs, or a 3000-gallon auxiliary fuel tank. The fourth bomb-bay was faired over, and it held 'ferret' electronic countermeasures (ECM) equipment to detect enemy radar and radio communications emissions, and allow the ECM operator to analyse them. RB-36s were identifiable visually by three radomes below the No 4 bomb-bay, and another beneath the nose for the 'ferret' antennae.

One of the aerial cameras tested in the first RB-36D (44-92088, redesignated ERB-36D) was the world's largest, the Boston University-designed K-42 'Pie Face' camera boasting a 240-inch focal length and a weight of three tons. Using negatives measuring 18 x 36 inches, it famously photographed a golf ball on a course from 45,000 ft and people in New York City's Central Park from 72 miles away. It occupied a considerable portion of the camera bay and required heated insulation.

Although the K-42 would obviously have been a very useful Cold War spying tool, severe problems with resolution caused by vibration limited its use in the ERB-36D to a single test programme. Like other strategic reconnaissance aircraft, the RB-36s were restricted to 'sniffer' patrols around the Soviet border – overflights of communist territory were the preserve of the Central Intelligence Agency. However, a 'Boston camera' would have provided imagery from deep within the communist bloc.

ECM protection was increasingly important for all bomber operations in the 1950s, and the B-36 was obviously a particularly conspicuous radar target. The B-model inherited a simple ECM set-up similar to the B-29's, but late B-36H/Js contained more comprehensive ECM arrangements than any other USAF aircraft at the time. This included an A-7 chaff dispenser that pumped out bundles five times larger than the usual versions.

The countermeasures equipment, installed by the supplying contractor and frequently updated, was initially offered as Group I or Group II using combinations of APT-1 and APT-4 transmitters and APR-4 receivers, depending on the likely radar threats for each type of mission. In 1954, Group III added an ALA-2 panoramic receiver and later APT-6 and APT-9 transmitters with APR-9 receivers. The AN/APS-54 radar warning receiver was introduced in B-36H/Js and retro-fitted to earlier versions. Further updates were added in the Featherweight programmes as ECM became increasingly important. RB-36s had additional ECM for their 'ferret' radar monitoring roles.

Four ECM operators controlled up to 34 receivers, recorders, analysers, tuners and radar cameras, among other devices. Each operator covered one frequency range. One dealt with low frequency emitters and doubled as a radio operator. Other positions concentrated their antennae on intermediate, medium or high frequency radars, with one operator dealing with each band to cover the full spectrum from 38 to 11,000 megacycles.

All 24 RB-36Ds (including seven that had originally been ordered as B-36Bs) were delivered to Rapid City (later, Ellsworth) AFB, South Dakota, which hosted the 28th BW's 72nd, 717th and 718th BSs. Its initial crews trained at Carswell before receiving their own aircraft from 8 July 1949. At first these were B-36Bs, but RB-36Ds had arrived by May 1951. It then became the 28th SRW, moving from the Fifteenth to the Eighth Air Force and becoming operational by June 1951.

Operating in temperatures as low as -40°F, the Rapid City wing maintainers welcomed the introduction of 'Luria' all-weather maintenance docks (extended versions of the Convair Maintenance Docks) to offer some protection for outdoor work in these conditions. Gloves were not an option for many of the delicate tasks, and at least one mechanic sustained severe frostbite when his hand became frozen to the interior of a B-36's wing. All crews suffered from the lack of heating in the aircraft's rear compartment, which became available only after take-off when the heat exchangers began to send hot air into the rear fuselage.

Frequent hailstorms damaged the fabric-covered control surfaces on early B-36s, and internal metal fuel lines contracted in the cold while their rubber hose connections did not, causing fuel leaks. Maintainers initially found the B-36 a maintenance nightmare after working on the B-29. They gradually reduced the maintenance man hours per flying hour ratio from 60-to-1 to 40-to-1, assisted by the provision of the base's 'Big Hangar' (the longest single-span structure in the world at the time) and an engine rebuild shop complete with an innovative engine analyser trouble-shooting device.

B-36Ds had a 15-man crew, including two radio operators, one of whom doubled as a gunner, as did the co-pilot and forward observer. The second radio man also managed the ECM equipment, a carry-over from the arrangement in B-29s. Five gunners worked in the rear compartment. New equipment included the radar and optical K-3A bombing/navigation system, which was installed in a modernisation programme to replace the somewhat unreliable K-1. These systems were still reliant on fragile vacuum tubes. A Y-3 periscopic bombsight replaced the Norden sight in many B-36Ds. Its small periscopic sight extended from the lower right forward fuselage, and the bomb-aimer's glazing was covered by aluminium.

FASTER AND HIGHER

In April 1949 the USAF decided on further investment in the 'Peacemaker', ordering 17 B-36Fs and 19 RB-36Fs, with a follow-on order for another

19 B-36Fs and five more reconnaissance versions in 1950. All were allocated to the 7th BW at Carswell AFB. The first example (49-2669) flew on 11 November 1950, introducing the more powerful R-4360-53 engine that could produce 3800 hp with water/alcohol injection, increasing the bomber's maximum speed to 417 mph and operational ceiling to 44,000 ft.

The new engine, with a pressurised crank case and an improved supercharger, was the only significant difference from the B/RB-36D specification. It also had a better reputation for oil retention. Clearly, development of the reciprocating engine was reaching a peak, but in service these massive powerplants became more reliable than earlier versions, partly due to the use of direct fuel injection and a revised low-tension ignition system. A proposal to use even more powerful R-4360-57 engines for additional B-36s was rejected in 1952 when it became clear that the B-52 would replace the B-36 as SAC's principal heavy bomber. RB-36Fs had a similar reconnaissance fit to the RB-36D. After its maiden flight on 30 April 1951, all 24 examples were in use with the four RB-36 wings by the end of 1951.

Two further contracts rounded off production, one of them delivering the most numerous variant, the B-36H. By September 1953 83 had been built, together with 73 RB-36Hs, which were similarly equipped to other RB-36s. Improvements included a revised bombing system code-named Blue Square, a reconfigured flightdeck, giving a position for a second flight engineer, and an updated tail gun sighting system in the form of the twin-radome AN/ANP-41A. Cockpit instrumentation was also improved.

B-36H performance figures matched those of the F-model, and it used the same engines, but with improved square-tipped propeller blades to reduce vibration at high altitudes. Two A-6 or A-7 dispensers with 1400 lbs of chaff were added to the B-36H and retrofitted to B-36Fs to boost their ECM capability against ever-improving hostile search radars.

ECM protection evolved through three series of installations designated Group I, II or III, depending on the combination of AN/APT-1, AN/APT-4, AN/APT-5A or later transmitters installed. Group III, installed from 1954, included an AN/ALA-2 panoramic receiver together with AN/APT-4, -6, -9 or -16 transmitters and an AN/APR-9 receiver. The B-36's capacious interior allowed it a far more comprehensive ECM suite than other contemporary bombers, giving the aircraft effective protection against contemporary Soviet radars. In RB-36s, the 'ferret' operator had a separate station in the rear compartment, and there were also operating stations for the intermediate and high frequency ECM equipment.

With 1950s technology and without automation, ECM was a very labour-intensive activity, and additions to the kit were made frequently. Late-production B-36Hs had wide-band AN/APS-54 radar warning receiver (RWR) equipment fitted in the nose glazing and at the root of the horizontal stabiliser to indicate whether the aircraft was being illuminated by enemy surface radar or by a radar-equipped fighter. It was the first RWR to be installed in a SAC bomber, and the AN/APS-54 soon became standard kit.

As Convair's final production model, the B-36J followed in July 1953. It included a few modifications to the B-36H format, specifically two extra fuel tanks in the outer wings that added 2770 gallons, increasing the total

RB-36F-15 50-1102 of the 99th SRW lifts off from Fairchild AFB with all ten engines generating their smoke trails. The six R-4360s and four J47s were set to take-off power, with the jets at 100 per cent. When lightly loaded, a B-36 accelerated fast. A firm backward pull on the control column by the pilot would make it climb at a rate of 2000-3000 ft per minute, allowing the bomber to attain an altitude of several thousand feet by the time the 'Peacemaker' reached the end of a lengthy SAC runway (*USAF*)

to 36,390 gallons. According to Convair, such a fuel load was sufficient to power a car around the globe 18 times. Fuel leaks, inherited from earlier versions, persisted, and groundcrews spent many hours removing hundreds of flat-head screws from wing panels so that they could purge, vent and reseal the wing tanks.

The J-model's reinforced landing gear allowed the maximum take-off weight to increase to a colossal 205 tons with only a 6 mph reduction in top speed. The last 14 of the 33 B-36Js delivered to the USAF were 'feather-weighted' by the removal of defensive armament and gunners in an attempt to give them extra altitude to evade the better-performing fighters that the Soviet Union was developing. Earlier J-models were also converted to Featherweight III configuration. For high-altitude missions above 43,600 ft, crews had to wear clumsy full-body pressure suits. Such flights were only undertaken on a few occasions, as the B-52 soon took over such high-altitude missions.

The final B-36J, 52-2827, was accepted by the 92nd BW on 20 August 1954. On 12 February 1959 it became the last B-36 to be retired from frontline service by the USAF when it flew out of Biggs AFB following its final flight with the 95th BW. During squadron service from Fairchild AFB, it was flown to 63,000 ft. Restored by volunteers after many years in open storage, the aircraft is currently on display at the Pima Air Museum in Arizona.

Although only 22 B-36s remained in service by the end of 1958, the final versions had corrected most of the mechanical and serviceability problems experienced by earlier examples. Aircraft availability had started at a low base, with less than ten of the 40 B-36s in service being serviceable at any one time in 1949. Through intensive service use, frequent updating and remanufacture and constantly refined maintenance procedures, the aircraft had become a reliable bearer of the nuclear deterrent by 1953. The US then had around 12,000 nuclear weapons and components stored in 23 countries around the world to supply its long-range bombers, with 'Albuquerque Station' at Kirtland AFB being the main US facility for the storage of both dummy and operational nuclear weapons.

CHAPTER FIVE

DOOMSDAY BOMBER

n its role as SAC's premier nuclear and long-range conventional bomber, the B-36 needed new mission profiles, operating strategies and weapons. On 20 September 1950, the 7th BW sent a B-36D from each of its three squadrons to fly a mission that followed SAC's Emergency War Order plan. It simulated a night attack on Fort Worth combined with a second bomb run across Birmingham, Alabama, complying with the idea that each nuclear attack would take out two targets.

The following month, the same 7th BW three-aircraft detachment was used to fly missions out of March and Castle AFBs in California to establish the feasibility of operations from forward locations. Requirements for support equipment, supplies and manpower were established. Indianapolis, in Indiana, was subjected to two simulated night strikes by 25 7th BW B-36s in mid-April 1951 as a test of tactics against a large industrial complex.

However, operational procedures for nuclear strikes could only be established via realistic tests with actual bombs. The USA conducted a series of atmospheric tests involving high-flying B-36s between 1952 and 1956, the 'Peacemakers' performing as bombers, atmospheric sampling platforms and photographic aircraft. The sampling (or 'effects') missions also collected radioactive material from nuclear tests by the Soviet Union and Britain.

The first such event, codenamed Operation *Ivy*, took place in August 1952 and required a full-scale rehearsal called Operation *Texas*, staged from

RB-36H-10 51-5743 deployed to Kirtland AFB for Operation *Teapot* in April 1955. During the bomb tests, a Mk 5 three-kiloton weapon was dropped from 46,000 ft to cause a high-altitude detonation. Two other B-36s then sampled the atmospheric debris from the resultant, massive smoke ring (*Terry Panopalis Collection*)

Bergstrom AFB, Texas. The latter involved 39 aircraft, including two B-36H bombers and a B-36D sampling and observation aircraft. A nuclear 'training shape' was dropped in the Gulf of Mexico, and the conditions for a real 500 kiloton Mk 18 bomb were simulated to ascertain the optimum speeds, drop altitudes and escape turns for the B-36. At the conclusion of the simulation it was still not clear whether the bombers would be able to escape the blast without being incinerated by radiation.

When the 'effects' B-36D during the actual *Ivy* flights conducted the first test (the *Mike* shot on 31 October 1952, using a Mk 5 thermonuclear device codenamed 'Sausage' detonated at Eniwetok atoll in the Pacific), it was almost caught in the mushroom cloud following the detonation, despite the aircraft being at 40,000 ft and 15 miles from the explosion. The bomber experienced very high temperatures and bending forces on its tail area. SAC had refused requests for a drogue parachute to be fitted to the bomb to slow its descent.

The second test, codenamed *King*, involved a Mk 18 weapon. Again, a rehearsal was conducted by an unmarked B-36H dropping a dummy Mk 18 near Eniwetok on 8 November 1952. One week later, the real Mk 18 was dropped from 40,000 ft, causing an apocalyptic 500 megaton explosion at the end of its 56-second fall. The B-36H completed its break-away turn, but still received blast damage and loads on its tail which approached the structural limits. This first series of tests brought about two B-36 modifications – the application of heat-reflective white paint on the undersides of the bomber and the installation of detachable aluminised asbestos shields inside the cockpit canopy to offer some measure of flash protection for the crew.

Carswell's 7th BW provided 12 B-36s for support of the oddly named Operations *Upshot-Knothole* and *Tumbler-Snapper* tests at the Nevada test site for nuclear weapons. They included dropping a lower-yield Mk 7 tactical bomb from a B-36 in order to help establish safe drop altitudes and measure shockwave stresses on the bomber's structure. The tests were followed in 1954 by Operation *Castle*, which involved several types of bomber including a Featherweight B-36, an RB-36 and the *Ivy* B-36D 'effects' aircraft.

The 'effects' B-36D-5 49-2653, commanded by Maj Frederick Bachmann of the 436th BS, was subjected to blast loads at altitudes up to 50,000 ft that reached its structural limits and damaged the bomb-bay, landing gear doors, radome and scanner blisters and the undersides of the engine nacelles. Considerable damage resulted from the scorching of the unpainted areas of the lower surfaces, some of which were subjected to temperatures of 322°F. Much of the protective white paint was stripped away, and gun turrets, propeller spinners and the crew communication tunnel were among many damaged components.

Upon its return to Carswell, the aircraft was found to be so radioactive that it was parked well away from other aircraft on base for a year to 'cool off'. When 49-2653 could finally be inspected in 1955, the airframe damage it had suffered was considered terminal and the bomber was scrapped. Other B-36s used in the tests were eventually decontaminated up to a year after their sampling flights.

Operation *Teapot* at the Nevada test site introduced parachute-retarded Mk 5 weapons dropped from a B-36 and detonating at around 46,600 ft.

Aircraft involved included RB-36H 51-5743 (RB-36Hs could reach 50,000 ft with all engines at full power), which expended three weapons – including 1.2 kiloton Mk 12s – during the 'Shot' portion of the 14 tests. The latter were to evaluate nuclear warheads for air defence use.

B-36s also served as support aircraft for the Operation *Redwing* test, which saw the first airdrop of a free-fall thermonuclear weapon. It took place at Eniwetok, with a B-52 as the delivery aircraft since the B-36 was considered too slow to make a safe escape. B-52B 52-013 was selected for the drop, rather than one of the four B-36Hs

from the 4925th Test Group (Atomic), although a 'Peacemaker' dropped the *Osage* XW-25 test warhead over Eniwetok on 16 June 1956. This event marked the end of the bomber's participation in the tests for the weapon it would have employed should war have broken out with the Soviet Union.

However, 5th SRW RB-36s fitted with four external sampling pods took part in the 90-day-long Operation *Miami Moon*, which saw three British nuclear weapons tested over Malden Island, in the Central Pacific, from May 1957. As the aircraft calibrated and sampled the nuclear clouds, a considerable quantity of radioactive material attached itself to their external surfaces, which required extensive washing at their temporary Hickam base after each flight.

5th SRW RB-36Hs were also used for Project Old Gold – the sampling of Soviet nuclear tests in the winter of 1957–58. The aircraft were based at Eielson AFB, Alaska, so that they could collect radioactive debris carried by the Arctic airstream from the Soviet test site.

While the B-36's record as a sampling and photographic aircraft for the tests was exemplary, the experience did cast doubts on its survivability as a high-altitude nuclear bomber. The 'Peacemaker's' weapons handbook was revised to advise an escape turn at 345 knots at 40,000 ft, but low-altitude delivery was also explored, as it was for other SAC bombers which, by 1956, faced much more effective enemy defences.

During Operation *Castle* a B-36 was flown at 500 ft to an initial point, where it 'popped up' to 16,000 ft to release a nuclear weapon at maximum speed, turned away at 45 degrees and then descended to 500 ft to escape. Low altitudes clearly put the bombers at more risk from a wide spectrum of anti-aircraft weapons, and range was inevitably reduced. Crew survival training allowed for escape and evasion tactics if they had to crash-land short of a safe border.

At least two 327th BS/92nd BW B-36Js from Fairchild AFB were fitted with atmospheric sampling boxes in place of the forward sighting blister behind their cockpits to collect irradiated airborne deposits after nuclear explosions. This aircraft, 52-2824, photographed in Hawaii, was one of four used for Operation Redwing in mid-April 1956 (Terry Panopalis Collection)

FITNESS FOR PURPOSE

In the mid-1940s the Joint Chiefs of Staff evolved a series of detailed strategies to counter Stalin's anticipated attempts to expand his empire, ranging from Operation *Broadview* (to defend the USA against a Soviet invasion) to Operation *Cockspur*, which saw Italy protected from invasion

SAC's nuclear strategy involved basing its B-36s as far north as possible. This 92nd BW aircraft takes on fuel in sub-zero Alaskan conditions in which the refuelling crew had to work on iced-over wings with minimal access equipment. Mechanics would have to climb onto the fuselage uppersurface and brave the slippery wing-walk areas to reach the engines between flights in order to perform routine servicing (*Terry Panopalis Collection*)

by the Red Army. The doomsday scenario of 1949's Operation *Bushwacker* included a massive nuclear air offensive to paralyse Soviet forces, while US ground armies were assembled for a conventional response in Europe or elsewhere. The build-up of SAC's B-36 and B-47 bomber armada was a key component of the *Bushwacker* strategy.

Among the more specific 'wargaming' scenarios was a contingency plan to counter an invasion of northeastern USA via Canada, requiring bombers to operate from bases as far north as possible. Attacks on the Soviet Union by bombers without in-flight refuelling would have to be made across the North Pole so that bases in the northeast USA, Alaska or Labrador were needed, rather than making extended flights from Carswell AFB in far-away Texas. Like other USAF aircraft, the B-36 had to be proofed against Arctic weather conditions and given more accurate means of navigation near the North Pole. This happened in 1949 in the Global Electronics Modification (GEM) programme. The latter also saw B-29s and B-50s fitted with in-flight refuelling equipment.

In September 1949 a 492nd BS B-36B flew to Eielson AFB to initiate the facility's use as a forward operating location for 'Peacemaker' training and operations. Eighteen B-36s from the 7th BW, with their tails and wingtips painted in the bright-red Arctic scheme for safety reasons, were subsequently deployed to Fairbanks AFB, Alaska, Goose Bay, Labrador, and Limestone AFB, Maine (built as the second B-36 base in 1947 and later re-named Loring), after B-36A 44-92007 was climate tested down to -72°F at Eglin AFB. The return flights to Carswell involved long detours over potential 'targets', and could take up to 33 hours to complete. B-36s could land on runways covered in two feet of snow if they were fitted with steel-studded snow tyres.

Preventing a B-36 from freezing up on the ground required the use of 18 Type F-1A heater units, blasting hot air into the engines and fuselage through long, flexible tubes. In summer heat at more southerly US bases, the same tubes were used to pump cool air through the aircraft. During Operation *North Star* in 1954, B-36s were required to maintain alert status and take off in temperatures of -40°F at Eielson AFB.

The extreme climatic conditions experienced in Alaska caused the second B-36 crash on 14 February 1950. Engine carburettor icing at 17,000 ft during a return flight to Carswell from an Alaskan cold weather exercise by ten GEM B-36Bs caused an unprecedented 'Broken Arrow' emergency situation. B-36B 44-92075 from the 7th BW had been ferried to Alaska by Col John D Bartlett, commander of the wing's 436th BS and project officer for the aircraft, and his crew. It arrived in snow, high winds and temperatures of -40°F. As the ninth B-36B on the 24-hour return flight to Carswell, 44-92075 was to be commanded by Capt Harold L Barry and his crew of 17.

On the southerly journey with B-36B 44-92083, the aircraft was to divert for an overflight of Fort Peck, Indiana, at 40,000 ft and then head cross-country to San Francisco for a simulated nuclear attack, before the final leg home to Fort Worth. Such long training flights were frequently undertaken in order to simulate the sorts of distances and altitudes that would be involved in attacks on Soviet targets.

Soon after take-off, Barry reported that ice had caused the inboard flaps to become stuck. As the bomber climbed into clouds, the propellers began to surge as they too became covered in ice – they now had to be controlled manually. At 12,000 ft, considerable icing probably accumulated on the wings too, and there was no provision for de-icing. Heating for the latter used hot engine air fed into chambers in both the wings' leading edges and the tail surfaces. It could be turned on if ice was anticipated, but prolonged use was thought to cause metal fatigue. 44-92075's de-icing equipment (which, in the B-36D, actually produced enough heat to supply 120 five-room houses, according to Convair) had been turned off earlier in the flight.

Seven hours into the flight Barry climbed to 15,000 ft to try and escape the icing, but the No 1 engine suddenly developed an intense fire, probably caused by ice choking off airflow to the carburettor and forcing it to run too rich on fuel. This in turn allowed highly flammable fuel to enter the hot exhaust system and cause a fire. The large Bendix-Stromberg carburettors, almost two feet wide, were somewhat ahead of the hot sections of the engine and susceptible to ice formation.

Moments later, the No 2 engine also caught fire and the propeller had to be feathered. Power in two more engines began to fail, and at 2325 hrs Barry had to send a distress signal via nearby B-36B 44-92083, saying that 'We are at 17,000 ft in severe icing. Instrument and engine trouble. Severe emergency. Going to let down through overcast to lose ice. Letting down

7th BW B-36H-50 52-1350 draws up its landing gear after take-off, displaying the white anti-flash Gloss White Enamel (MIL-E-7729) applied under Technical Order 1B-36-895 of 4 February 1955. Borders of the white areas were feathered. This example lacks the 50-inch fuselage national insignia – the underwing 'star and bars' have also been deleted, which became routine practice when white anti-flash paint was introduced. 52-1350 does, however, have the twin AN/APG-41 tail gun radar in a single radome (*USAF*)

due to icing and an engine fire. Alerted crew to bail out but may ditch'. He was apparently intending to ditch the bomber near Queen Charlotte Island off the coast of British Columbia.

Although the fires were extinguished the B-36 continued to lose altitude, forcing Barry to order the crew to bail out into near-freezing rain and a howling gale. They struggled to remove their parachutes and 'Mae West' life preservers in order to don exposure suits under these survival items. Weaponeer Capt Ted Schreier went into the bomb-bay to disarm the Mk 4 nuclear bomb that they carried – the first time he had performed this complex task in flight.

By midnight all trace of the aircraft had disappeared, and 44-92083, patrolling overhead for an hour, was unable to re-establish contact or work out exactly where the B-36 had gone down. Operation *Brix* – a search effort by more than 40 aircraft, including US Navy P2V Neptunes and a US Coast Guard PBY Catalina, together with Royal Canadian Air Force aircraft and the Royal Canadian Navy destroyer HMCS *Cayuga* – began immediately in dreadful weather conditions. Numerous other vessels, USAF B-29s (one of which crashed after take-off with the loss of eight crew) and an H-5 helicopter were also called in for a wide survey around the Vancouver Island area.

On the second day of the search 11 survivors were gradually located on Princess Royal Island after wisps of campfire smoke were noticed by a fishing boat. A 12th, engineer 1Lt Charles Pooler, was found the following day some distance away with a broken ankle, but it was assumed that the other five men (the first group to leave the aircraft) had bailed out over water before the B-36 crossed the island and had drowned in the rough, icy seas. After eight days only scattered survival kit debris had been found, and the search was called off.

The question of the bomber's final location, and that of its 11,000-lb Mk 3 'Fat Man' atom bomb, or bombs, remained. Several rescued crew members and local people recalled seeing the B-36 pass over them more than once in a shallow turn, rather than heading southwest into the Pacific on autopilot to crash, as Barry had intended. Crucially, extreme security measures by the US government meant that it was not clear whether the weapon, the first to be lost, had its multi-million-dollar, 13-lb plutonium core installed, rather than a lead dummy. The fear remained that the weapon could have landed on Canadian territory undetected, or it could possibly have been recovered by a Soviet vessel. The USAF stated that it had been jettisoned and destroyed at sea by its own high explosive 'lenses' before the bomber ditched.

The discovery of the bomber's semi-intact wreckage three years later at 5800 ft on snow-covered Mount Kologet in the Kispiox Valley (known as 'The Hidden Place') over 200 miles northeast of its supposed ditching location deepened the mystery. Very swift action by the USAF to reach the almost inaccessible crash site and dynamite the wreck suggested the possible presence of nuclear items still on board, or at least an urgent endeavour to remove or destroy classified equipment.

Although the possibility remained that a lightened fuel load and melted ice on the wings, three engines set at full throttle and a self-adjusted autopilot might have enabled the aircraft to achieve that distance and altitude when it had seemed about to fall out of the sky, other theories were suggested. One was that weaponeer Schreier, a qualified third pilot and the only crewman who was not seen to bail out, may have stayed on board and flown the bomber in search of a safe landing strip. Indeed, there were reports that the bomber had intended to attempt a landing at Terrace, in British Columbia.

When the wreckage was found, it appeared that the B-36 had been deliberately stalled into a low-speed belly flop landing, wheels down, in a deep snow field on the mountain side. Later visitors to the site concluded that most of the damage to the aircraft had been caused by the USAF's demolition charges, rather than a crash.

As for Schreier, apart from an unused parachute and rumours that his ID dog-tags had been found, there was no clear evidence of his fate. Streets at Carswell AFB were named after four of the lost crew. No such honour was bestowed upon Schreier, however.

THE BOMB

Paralleling the GEM adaptations, 52 B-36s were modified over three years from 1947 to carry the early Mk 3 'Fat Man' nuclear device in Project Saddle Tree. This was followed by Project On Top to carry other nuclear bombs, including the Mks 4, 5 and 6 versions. The Mk 4, tested in 1948, had an inner and outer spherical charge of three tons of high explosive and a plutonium core with layers of uranium and plutonium in a nickel jacket, suspended in a uranium sphere. A small beryllium and polonium 'urchin' sphere inside the core initiated the reaction process by releasing neutrons that caused fission to occur within the core, which would have been liquidised by the detonation of the conventional explosives.

To preserve a degree of safety, the core was not inserted into the weapon before flight. This process, taking up to 30 minutes to complete, required a technician (the 'weaponeer') and his bomb commander supervisor to work within the severely cold, unpressurised bomb-bays, removing several components from the bomb's interior. He then inserted the core components from their 'bird cage' secure carriage device into the weapon with special tools, including a rod 30 inches long. Later, in 1951, automatic motor-driven methods were used for the insertion and extraction of the core.

All cores and handling equipment were owned by the Atomic Energy Commission and 'loaned' to SAC under conditions of extreme security. Loading the weapon took place behind black curtains after it was transported to the flightline in a convoy of vehicles accompanied by two jeeps armed with 0.50-cal machine guns. For a time, security at some SAC bases was so strict, particularly after the Korean War began, that all personnel servicing B-36s or working in control rooms had to carry side-arms – often their own personal pistols.

A UBS system was developed so that several types of weapons up to 11 ft long could be selected to hang in the No 1 bomb-bay, or in all four bays of many B-36D/Hs. Other models had UBS by 1956, with standardised installation in the Nos 1 and 4 bays for all models, but with various alternative combinations. With the arrival of the 18.5-ft-long TX-14 and TX-17/Mk 17 'Runt' hydrogen bombs in 1951, later B-36s were gradually

The 18.5-ft-long TX-14 and TX-17/Mk 17 'Runt' hydrogen bombs were the largest and most powerful thermonuclear weapons ever deployed by US armed forces. Late-build B-36s were modified to carry this 20-megaton weapon (*USAF*)

modified to carry this fearsome 20-megaton weapon, or the dummy versions ('shapes' or 'skins', weighing the same as a real weapon). For foreign deployments, UBS bays could also be used to carry bicycles or low-powered motor bikes, which had become standard transport methods for maintainers to travel between the various parts of the vast SAC bases.

By the end of their careers, B-36s had been through an unprecedented number of modification and improvement programmes. The 1953 Project SAM-SAC was a four-year series of deep maintenance cycles that sought to impose a standard configuration on the B-36 fleet to simplify replacement of parts and maintenance routines. This undertaking occupied up to 5800 Convair employees at Fort Worth who inspected airframes, resealed fuel tanks, fitted new parts and performed a multitude of other procedures on 13 aircraft per month.

By 1957, at least 25 B-36s were in deep maintenance at any one time. Lacking enough hangars (despite some being built in the mid-1950s) to accommodate the bombers, Convair developed 36-ft-long maintenance docks that fitted over the wing to the width of three engines. Combinations of docks, which were either fixed or moveable, could be used to service all six engines, the landing gear and any systems within the wings. They had inbuilt heating, lighting and electrical connections. Another type of dock covered the nose and cockpit areas.

TEN-MINUTE TEXAS TORNADO

The B-36 never faced the fury of Soviet air defences, but Mother Nature managed to put more than half of the B-36 force out of action in just ten minutes, forcing Gen LeMay to temporarily remove the Carswell wing's controlling 19th Air Division (AD) from the SAC war plan.

On 1 September 1952, dark storm clouds began moving rapidly towards Fort Worth at 1800 hrs, with winds reaching 91 mph and gusting to 125 mph. Fortunately, most personnel were off-base for the Labor Day holiday. B-36s parked at Carswell and at the Convair facility were blown into, or onto, each other. Fuel gushed out over the dispersal areas and power at the base had to be cut off to avoid electrical lines from igniting disastrous fires. Ten minutes later the winds subsided. The carnage now became evident, although there were no serious injuries to personnel.

No fewer than 72 B-36s were reported as destroyed at Carswell, and another 24 at Fort Worth. In all, 106 had to be taken out of service. Many had their tails torn off, and considerable damage to aircraft and buildings was caused by the B-36 maintenance docks being picked up by the tempest and smashed into them. Incredibly, there were no fires, despite most of the aircraft having

The only total loss from the Carswell tornado in September 1952 was B-36D-10 44-92051, which was blown into an adjacent field and torn apart. Much of the wreckage was salvaged or used in the repair of other damaged bombers (*USAF*)

been fuelled up for the following day's planned mass deployment to North Africa.

This ruinous damage to America's strategic defence simply had to be repaired expeditiously, and a massive effort supervised by Brig Gen Clarence 'Bill' Irvine, by then commander of the 19th AD, began immediately. Because the concentration of bombers was so close to the Convair plant, inspection and assessment of the damage by a company team headed by Tom Neely and Air Materiel Command's San Antonio Air Materiel Area could be organised quickly. Neely identified ten aircraft that had slight to moderate damage, and they were tackled immediately. Within a week the first aircraft, B-36H 50-1096, had the wide gashes in its fuselage and other damage repaired at a cost of more than half-a-million dollars and it was returned to its squadron. The remaining nine bombers were repaired within two weeks.

Seriously damaged Carswell examples could be moved to the Convair factory for repair or remanufacture, and 19 were effectively rebuilt there. In Project Fixit, 26 aircraft were assigned to Convair for extensive remanufacture and repair. The original Fixit cost estimate exceeded $48m. Repairs proceeded rapidly, and production of the necessary components such as vertical tail assembly fixtures was considerably increased.

Damage to tails and rear fuselages was the most common problem. It was soon apparent that the losses were not as severe as it first seemed. In the end, only one aircraft, B-36D 44-92051, was a total loss, having been blown all the way into an adjacent field, with its tail and left wing ripped off and its fuselage fractured. The hulk went to New Mexico for the Sandia Laboratory's secret nuclear radiation tests.

Within ten days of the disaster, the 7th BW had enough aircraft to resume operations, and by the end of September its complement of operational B-36s actually exceeded the total before the tornado. The last repair job was completed by 11 May 1953. One B-36H (51-5712) was considered beyond repair for operational use, as its cockpit and nose area were smashed. It was duly converted into the NB-36H nuclear testbed aircraft in 1954 with a revised nose section. The aircraft subsequently undertook extensive trials with an airborne nuclear reactor as a power source.

To prevent similar losses in future, Carswell introduced a policy of overnight dispersal to other airfields, including Davis-Monthan AFB, in Arizona, and Biggs AFB whenever Texas storms appeared to be threatening its 'Peacemakers'.

A powerful tornado hit Puerto Rico in 1956, and the 72nd BW was able to evacuate most of its RB-36s in time. Unflyable examples were turned into the wind with their engines running as the eye of the storm passed over Ramey AFB and no aircraft were lost. However, 6th BW B-36J 52-2818 was apparently caught in a tornado forming at 25,000 ft over West Texas on 25 May 1955 while airborne. The left wing was broken off and the aircraft crashed near Sterling City with the loss of Capt L C Basinger and his 15-man crew.

7th BW aircraft B-36D-1 44-92097 and B-36H-5 50-1096 were forced to collide by the storm. Both were repaired, although 44-92097 was lost in another accident in August 1954 (*USAF*)

CHAPTER SIX

GLOBAL REACH

B-36B-5 44-92042 was modified for filming radar gun tests against intercepting F-80 fighters in 1949. As a B-36D, it visited snowy Britain in January 1952, landing short of the runway at RAF Boscombe Down with very little damage. The open upper rear gun compartment allowed the crew to escape (*NARA*)

In 1949 SAC began to deploy its expanding B-36 force outside the USA. On 24 May, four 7th BW aircraft led by Brig Gen Clarence Irvine flew from Carswell to Ramey AFB. Deployments increased in 1951, with six B-36s from the 11th BW making the 5000-mile flight to the French Moroccan air base at Sidi Slimane on 2 December for five days. They were supported by C-124 Globemaster II transports of the 1st Strategic Support Squadron. The asphalt ramps at the base had only recently been laid, and the fully loaded B-36s began to sink into the soft surfaces, which were weakened by spilled fuel, when they were parked and refuelled. Six bases in French Morocco were made available to SAC, with Sidi Slimane and Ben Guerir open to bombers.

Eleven months earlier, 11 B-36Ds had flown to RAF Lakenheath from Carswell via Limestone AFB for a week to establish operational procedures for the aircraft from a British base. En route, a night bombing attack was simulated over the Heligoland range in West Germany, and four more realistic training missions were later flown from Lakenheath.

At least 12 staging exercises by B-36s were flown from US bases as part of Emergency War Plan (EWP) exercises that involved other USAFE units supervised by the 7th AD, recovering to British bases including RAF Brize Norton, Upper Heyford, Fairford and Sculthorpe, between January 1951 and October 1956. Each visit was supported by three C-124s full of parts and equipment, together with 128 personnel. West German 'targets' were used for simulated attacks by aircraft flying from the USA and staging to a British base, before returning home.

The first British deployment to Lakenheath for Operation *United Kingdom* in January 1951 used three B-36Ds from the 7th and 11th BWs. The second Lakenheath excursion by three Carswell B-36Ds included an appearance at the Paris Air Show on 1 July 1951 following an overflight of London by the thunderous trio.

B-36s had actually appeared over Britain as early as 1948 for simulated combat, including interceptions by RAF nightfighters that showed the bomber was able to survive well if flown at night or in bad weather with full use of its ECM. In daylight, with uninterrupted radar control, the fighters stood a better chance. It was assumed at the time that the Soviet Union was far short of establishing an effective radar network to cover its vast terrain.

During one of the 1951 deployments Meteor F 8s of No 245 Sqn practised interceptions, but they did not include head-on attacks in case the fighters, at high closing speeds, hit the B-36's lofty vertical tail. In rear attacks, fighter pilots had to use the bomber's horizontal tail to set their gunsights for range, rather than the usual wingspan setting, as their gunsight calibrations were limited to a 140-ft wingspan. Like USAF pilots of early gun-armed jets, the RAF pilots found it difficult to approach close enough to the bombers at high altitude from the rear without being thrown out of control by the formidable 'prop-wash'.

It was also clear that the B-36's gun turrets had them covered during attacks from other angles. In later years, the gunners had difficulty in tracking faster fighters at close range, as did their B-29 counterparts when fending off MiG-15s during the Korean War.

A handful of 'Peacemakers' were lost either while on deployment in Britain or on their way home. The first of these was B-36D 49-2658, which crashed following a mid-air collision with a F-51D Mustang on 27 April 1951 during its return flight to the USA from a deployment to Lakenheath. Details of this accident can be found in the next chapter.

On 7 February 1953, B-36H 51-5719 from the 492nd BS/7th BW was caught in bad weather over Britain while heading for Fairford for Operation *Styleshow* with 16 other 'Peacemakers'. Strong tailwinds across the Atlantic saw the bomber reach its destination three hours ahead of its scheduled time of arrival, but the mission brief did not allow for an early

RB-36D-10 49-2689 of the 28th SRW (which deployed repeatedly to forward bases) at Rapid City – later Ellsworth – AFB. With 23 cameras, 'ferret' ECM equipment and 80 flash bombs to occupy its crew of 18 or more, the RB-36D was a formidable reconnaissance platform (*USAF*)

landing and the crew had to loiter overhead until their specified arrival time. By then Fairford, famous for its thick fogs, was 'socked in' with very low cloud, and the base's landing control radar was limited to handling one aircraft every 15 minutes, but it had 17 B-36s in the approach circuit.

Denied the chance of a diversionary airfield, 51-5719 eventually ran short of fuel after its second failed ground-controlled approach (GCA) and the 13-man crew had to abandon the aircraft. All were recovered safely, having come down in Oxfordshire, Berkshire and Wiltshire. The bomber flew on for another 30 miles before crashing in a farmer's field near the village of Lacock, in Wiltshire.

B-36H 51-5729, displaying the 'triangle J' tail markings of the 7th BW, was another casualty of the EWP deployments to Britain. Returning from Fairford on 12 February 1953, the crew received inaccurate GCA information from Goose Bay and the bomber crashed into a forested hillside, killing two crew in a rear compartment.

The following month, on 18 March, RB-36H 51-13721 from the 28th SRW at Rapid City AFB and its crew were lost while returning from a training flight to Lajes AFB in the Azores. Approaching Random Island, off the Newfoundland coast near St John's, at an altitude of 1000 ft, they were scheduled to test the Eastern Defense Command's radar systems in Exercise Round Out. The aircraft's navigator lost his bearings due to unexpectedly strong tailwinds, which placed them over land ten minutes sooner than expected. Flying on instruments in freezing fog and sleet, with two jet engines stopped by ice, the aircraft hit Random Island at 200 knots, spreading wreckage over hundreds of feet of the frozen terrain.

Among the 23 fatalities was Brig Gen Richard E Ellsworth, the popular and highly respected base commander at Rapid City AFB and a veteran of the China-India-Burma theatre in World War 2. He had assumed command of the 28th SRW from Col Albert Wilson on 15 November 1950. On 13 June 1953, President Dwight D Eisenhower renamed the 28th SRW's home Ellsworth AFB in his honour.

On 5 August 1953, whilst on deployment from Travis AFB to Lakenheath, RB-36H 52-1369 of the 5th SRW experienced loss of power. It was ditched in the Atlantic west of Scotland, but only four of the 19-man crew survived.

There were also some close shaves for B-36 crews flying from British airfields, and these were primarily caused by poor weather. On 27 January 1952, 7th BW B-36D 44-92042, which already had three piston engines and one J47 jet shut down following inflight failures, was heading for Boscombe Down when it ran into a heavy snowstorm. Seeing the recently installed aircraft warning lights atop the 404-ft spire of nearby Salisbury Cathedral, the pilot circled around the area to reduce the fuel load to a safe landing limit. He then saw other lights, which he apparently mistook for the approach lights at Boscombe Down. The bomber landed short in a snow-covered field alongside the A303 trunk road with minimal damage. It was towed across to a dispersal ramp at Boscombe Down, cleaned up and flown back to Ellsworth AFB with a different pilot at the helm.

Another Carswell B-36H (51-5742) deploying to Fairford in February 1953 was almost lost when it suffered severe technical problems en route.

The crew had been briefed to hit sea targets south of England with simulated nuclear shapes whilst flying to Fairford from Texas. As night fell, they passed Iceland and headed for Britain, starting the jet engines and commencing a climb to a typical bombing altitude of 46,000 ft.

At 42,400 ft all ten engines suddenly cut out, the lights went off and long flames streamed from the J47 pods where raw fuel was still entering the hot combustion chambers. Pilot Capt Richard S George noted that the aircraft had 'the glide characteristics of a streamlined crowbar'. Both flight engineers, Ed Kieschnik and Robert Hardwick, worked frantically on the alternators to try and restore electrical power, and as the aircraft 'glided' down to 37,600 ft they managed to get several reciprocating engines re-started.

Arriving safely at Fairford, the B-36 was subjected to a thorough examination. No fault was found and the apprehensive crew were told to fly back to Carswell via Goose Bay, although a further problem with propeller reverse switching had to be solved following the pre-flight checks. At Carswell a deeper inspection found that a loose nut inside a bomb-bay electrical panel had shorted out the main electrical bus, but the obstruction had eventually burned out so that current could flow again, enabling some engines to be re-started.

Lethal accidents could occur on even the most routine training flights. 28th SRW RB-36H 51-13722 was flying practice landing approaches to Ellsworth AFB on the night of 27 August 1954 when, on the sixth approach, pilot Capt Neil Williams let the bomber's left wing hit a ground warning light display on top of low hills northwest of the runway. The crew had been warned that the lights were inoperative, but a mis-calibrated ground control approach radar at the base added to the problems. The RB-36H disintegrated, killing 26 of the 27 crew on board.

DAYS IN THE AIR

During the B-36 units' regular flights of at least 24 hours, the crews tended to operate in four-hour shifts with four-hour breaks, the latter being taken either in the rear fuselage bunks or in hammocks slung in the rear section of the forward crew area. Although their normal operational stations were in the 'glasshouse' nose, the navigator, radar observer and other observers had to sit in the radio room, facing aft with their backs against the bulkhead, for take-off.

With all ten engines running and unencumbered by bombs and a full fuel load, the B-36 was surprisingly sprightly on take-off. However, with full fuel and heavy weapons loads, the crew would not attempt take-off if one or more engines were not developing full power. The aircraft's three pilots and three navigator/radar operators were the most vital crew members, and they relied on gunners to bring them hot food from the galley while taking it in turns to man key stations in the cockpit and 'glasshouse' nose. SAC rules stated that the first pilot was the aircraft commander, the co-pilot was known as the pilot and the third pilot would double up as a weaponeer or in some other role.

It was also SAC policy to keep crews together where possible, and LeMay was happy to use the promotion system to retain crews as working units. Each crew would be scheduled for one of these long missions at roughly ten-day intervals. They had targets, weapons and routes allocated in

In keeping with its strategy of self-sufficiency, SAC experimented with external pods to carry spare R-4360 engines to forward operating bases. B-36B-1 44-92026 (seen here) was one of two B-models that were suitably modified to carry pods attached to the racks in their forward bomb-bays (*USAF*)

advance so that briefing was unnecessary. The final task pre-flight was an urgent visit to the latrines, as most crewmen tried to avoid using the 'honey bucket' toilets on board the aircraft, mainly because anyone who did so had to clean them out after the flight.

Targets were defined in terms of flight time and bearing, rather than by named cities. Top secret libraries of target information were kept at forward bases like Andersen AFB, on Guam. Landing grounds on return were not necessarily the home base – some crews were expected to return to an airfield in Iran. Dhahran, in Saudi Arabia, was occasionally used, and crews had to protect their aircrafts' transparencies and observation blisters from blasting by sandstorms at that location. Crews on alert status were expected to be airborne within five minutes of the alarm signal.

Pre-flighting the aircraft was included in the 24-hour timescale and it included jobs for all the crew. Gunners could be called on to perform a range of difficult tasks, including assisting with manually lowering the main landing gear if it failed to drop down when activated in flight. After climbing out into the wing on a catwalk, a pair of crewmen (usually gunners) could access the open gear well through a zippered flap at its edge. From there, they could operate the down-lock mechanism by kicking downwards against it to make it lock manually at low altitude.

Pilot Lt Col Ed Sandin of the 5th SRW pioneered a hazardous technique for reaching down and inserting a main landing gear down-lock in flight after numerous attempts to make the gear lock down. The narrow crawl-way to this position over the wheel well meant that the job had to be done without wearing a parachute, while trying to avoid looking down into an open abyss below.

GUARDIANS OF THE UPPER REALMS

The October 1951 visit to Sculthorpe, a highly classified lair in Norfolk for numerous intelligence-gathering aircraft, was the first by RB-36 reconnaissance aircraft. Seven RB-36Ds from the 28th SRW – the first of four SAC RB-36-equipped strategic reconnaissance wings – made the type's first operational visit to Europe to test pre-strike staging. While deployed, they flew a round-trip simulated photo-reconnaissance and strike mission to Morocco that included a parachute drop of target imagery files on Heathrow Airport for processing at a technical centre in West Drayton.

Twelve months later, the 28th SRW entered three crews in SAC's newly instigated Reconnaissance, Photo and Navigation Competition, competing with RB-50s and RB-45s. The 28th SRW won, securing the Paul T Cullen Trophy. Four RB-36s from the 5th SRW competed the following year, winning the Cullen Trophy again, while the 92nd BW entrants beat B-50, B-29 and B-47 crews to win the Muir S Fairchild Trophy for the first time. For 1954, the year in which B/RB-36 numbers in service peaked with 342 aircraft in ten wings, 'Peacemaker' crews won the top three places. The RB-36 entrants in that year's Reconnaissance and Navigation Competition secured the top prizes in all six categories, beating RB-47s. The more numerous Stratojet crews began to display better form in 1955, securing the Muir S Fairchild Trophy, with the RB-36 wings having reverted to bombing roles.

In 1956, within a much-expanded version of the event, the B/RB-36s of the 26th and 98th BW(H)s and the 11th BW won the Fairchild Trophy, beating B-47s and the newly introduced B-52s that would quickly displace the 'Peacemakers' in heavy bomb wings. Two crews, one from the 26th BS commanded by Capt P J O'Malley and another from the 98th BS with Lt Col J H Seely as commander, each flew three simulated missions from Loring AFB. Marks were awarded for navigation (on this occasion often in bad weather) and accuracy in simulated bombing on a radar bomb scoring area. The navigators' basic traditional skills in using a sextant to obtain fixes from stars were proven once again to be as vital in their success as were those of the radar observers.

The lower flightdeck of RB-36H-5 50-1110. 1Lt James Shively (lower left) occupies the navigator's chair, with photo-navigator Capt William Merrill to his right. Capt Franklin O'Donald (radar observer) peers into his 'scope to Shively's rear and A1C Albert Brown sits beside Merrill acting as nose gunner and weather observer (*NARA*)

B-36s did compete in the sixth competition in 1957, but they were already outnumbered by B-52s and the main awards all went to Stratojet crews. The seventh in the series of competitions in October 1958 marked the last appearance by the RB-36, with only 33 aircraft remaining in SAC after a very rapid reduction in numbers. Just two aircraft, operating from Castle AFB, participated. The top three prizes were taken by the 26 participant B-47 crews.

From November 1952 RB-36Hs of the 5th and 28th SRWs flew photo-reconnaissance missions in Operation *Roundabout*, which had previously been undertaken by RB-50Es of the 38th SRS from Sculthorpe and Mildenhall. The RB-36Hs flew from Upper Heyford and Fairford, and rotated through other British bases – there were, for example, up to eight aircraft at Lakenheath in August 1953. Their highly classified missions took them to within a safe distance of the borders of communist bloc countries to gather electronic information (ELINT) and take photographs, as well as rehearsing their nuclear strike capability. Some of these flights, lasting for 32 hours, involved seven-hour patrols beyond the Aleutian Islands photographing airfields more than 200 miles into Soviet territory from 44,000 ft, this altitude lending them some safety from MiG-15s.

The nuclear task eventually took priority, as it did in other RB-36 wings, in 1955, when the 28th became a Bomb Wing (Heavy). It took part in the regular B-36 rotational deployments to Guam, operating from Andersen AFB between April and July 1955 and for regular summer deployments thereafter. Strategically, this base put B-36s within striking range of most Soviet cities. All four B-36 wings rotated through Guam annually, partly to deter the communist Chinese from threatening the islands of Matsu and Quemoy in the Taiwan Strait. RB-36Hs of the 5th SRW were placed on maximum alert status in February and March 1955 on Guam, and some were loaded with incendiary bombs for a possible attack on China.

The tropical conditions on the island made corrosion a constant problem. Guns rusted quickly, requiring daily cleaning and oiling. The large area occupied by the parking dispersal on Guam required many squadrons to take their own lightweight vehicles, strapped to pallets in the bomb-bays, so that they could get to their aircraft more easily.

At least one 28th SRW mission took an RB-36 crew on a 32-hour flight across the Aleutian Islands at 44,000 ft. For seven hours the aircraft's 11 cameras probed 200 miles into Soviet territory, securing images of airfields and military installations. On return, the imagery was delivered to Offutt AFB, in Omaha, for analysis. Similar missions explored Chinese airfields from a safe distance. In 1957 B-52s were acquired and the last B-36 left Ellsworth on 29 May.

By 1953 several SAC units had re-equipped or been renamed, including the 5th BW at Travis AFB whose early reconnaissance missions in RB-29s had mapped Soviet and Chinese radar defences from covert positions around those countries' borders. During their long-range missions, crews had detected gaps in the Soviet Union's radar chain between Alaska and Murmansk and in the Bering Strait area between North America and Siberia. This information opened up obvious potential attack routes for SAC bombers, and the reconnaissance missions were continued after the wing received RB-36Ds while Col Walter E Arnold was commander. The 5th BW's first two 'Peacemakers' had arrived in January 1951, and B-36Js were received later. In September 1958 the wing, whose Hawaiian motto was 'Kiai O Ka Lewa' ('Guardians of the Upper Realms'), began transitioning to the B-52.

The three squadrons of the 6th BW converted from B-29s to B-36Fs at Walker AFB, near Roswell, New Mexico, in August 1952 as the 6th BW(H), losing the 307th Aerial Refuelling Squadron (ARS) and its KB-29Ps in the process, as they were not required for B-36 operations. The wing's hot-and-high desert base was unique in having a vast hangar that could house three B-36s. Despite Walker's location, crews usually had to take full arctic survival gear aboard, as any mission might be diverted to an unexpected destination. The wing deployed to Andersen AFB from October 1955 to January 1956, by which time it had acquired some Featherweight III B-36Js. B-52s became available in 1957, and the B-36s were phased out during August of that year.

In January 1953, the Pennsylvania Air National Guard's 111th SRW, which had been activated during the Korean War, became the 99th SRW at Fairchild AFB as one of SAC's four B-36-equipped strategic reconnaissance wings. It initially retained the 111th's RB-29s, although these were soon replaced by RB-36Fs. The wing continued to perform the worldwide photo-reconnaissance and ELINT role as its primary mission until the former

The 92nd BW refines its formation tactics for long-distance deployments. Early B-36A/B formations were flown partly as propaganda displays to disguise the lack of serviceable machines, but nuclear roles generally involved just one aircraft (*USAF*)

was relegated to a secondary mission in 1956. It flew similar intelligence-gathering missions around the fringes of Soviet territory to the operations managed by the 28th SRW.

The 99th SRW deployed aircraft to Andersen AFB from January to April 1956, replacing the 6th BW, but in September of that year the wing was redesignated as the 99th BW(H) and it converted to the B-52C, operating from Westover AFB, Massachusetts. As a B-36 wing, the 99th was best known for its participation in the Fighter-Conveyer (FICON) parasite fighter project.

WEST TO EAST

The first deployment of a whole wing of B-36s outside the USA was made in Operation *Big Stick* – a post-Korean War show of strength to the North Korean peace negotiators and their Soviet and Chinese supporters during August–September 1953 by the 92nd BW, commanded by Col James V Edmundson. The aircraft made the 6500-mile journey in five-aircraft cells (with one of three bombers), totalling 23 B-36s. Carrying dummy Mk 6 atomic weapons, their navigation was sent awry by bad weather as they approached Kadena AB, on Okinawa, in an area where air traffic radar control was virtually non-existent. The cells were dispersed, with some B-36s flying dangerously close to the Soviet-occupied Kamchatka Peninsula.

'Peacemakers' were sent for 30 days to Okinawa, Japan and Guam, with the latter site also being a storage field for nuclear weapons. As previously noted, B-36 wings rotated their squadrons through Guam annually, where aircraft were sometimes put on alert loaded with incendiary bombs.

Based at Fairchild AFB, the 92nd BW's 325th, 326th and 327th BSs also made the first deployment to Andersen AFB by an entire B-36 wing, giving them access to a massive area of terrain bordering the Pacific Ocean. Their first migration to the island was between 15 October 1954 and 12 January 1955, and the whole wing revisited in three-aircraft 'cells' for a 90-day deployment from 25 April to 6 July 1957.

The 92nd BW had a legacy of records from World War 2, having been the first Eighth Air Force bomb group to cross the Atlantic for operations from Britain in 1942. It subsequently became the last bomb group to fly a combat mission with the 'Mighty Eighth' during the conflict. The unit exchanged its B-29s for B-36s from 20 July 1951, becoming the 92nd BW(H) rather than a medium bomb wing – all B-29 'heavy' bomber wings were reclassified as 'medium' when the appreciably larger B-36 arrived.

Among the last 'Peacemaker' units to form was the 42nd BW at Loring AFB, this site having been massively expanded by SAC

B-36Ds of the 92nd BW from Fairchild AFB flew to Okinawa in August 1953 for Operation *Big Stick* – the first large-scale 'Peacemaker' deployment abroad under SAC's EWP. Fifteen flew via Eielson in cells of three, while five weight-reduced examples (the 'Featherweight Force') flew direct from Fairchild AFB, visiting other 'targets' en route. Despite disruptive weather conditions, all arrived safely (*NARA*)

One of the 92nd BW's 'Peacemakers' being prepared for towing by a Far East Air Force-owned 'mule' tractor during the wing's visit to Yokota AB on 28 August 1953. *Big Stick* showed that US armed forces had a continuing Far East commitment after the Korean War (*Terry Panopalis Collection*)

from a small radar station. Its low winter temperatures, with frequent snowdrifts four feet deep, meant that all the main buildings had to be linked by underground tunnels. The aircraft tyres had metal staples embedded in them to provide some grip on runways covered in a foot of ice. The 42nd BW began training on the B-36 from April 1953 under Col Frederick B Ramputi, and its three squadrons, the 69th, 70th and 75th BS, were combat ready by 7 January 1954 with assistance from the 7th BW at Carswell AFB.

Landing on icy runways was a hazard in itself. B-36D 49-2653 had to return to Loring after it encountered a severe snowstorm, and despite pilot Capt Leno Pezzato's best efforts, the bomber skidded on landing and the wing dug into a snowbank. The aircraft then burst into flames, and several crew in the rear compartment suffered burns.

The 42nd BW soon began deployments to Britain, sending detachments to Burtonwood and Upper Heyford. One aircraft managed to reach Burtonwood in September 1954 with only two of its reciprocating engines developing power. The whole wing was at Upper Heyford for a month from 18 October 1955. At its chilly base in the northeastern USA, the 42nd BW also hosted the 42nd ARS with its KC-97Gs, although these tankers were used to refuel B-47 Stratojets crossing the Atlantic.

On 14 August 1954 the 42nd BW received the last B-36 (a J-model) to be delivered to SAC, and its relatively short time with the 'Peacemaker' ended in September 1956. It was the first B-36 wing to convert to the B-52, becoming the second SAC wing to operate the Stratofortress and the first to convert to it from a propeller-driven type.

B-36s had equipped 11 SAC wings, and the bomber was unique in carrying the full range of nuclear weapons, including the huge Mk 17. However, by the mid-1950s, it was clear that the 'Peacemaker's' operational life would be curtailed by its increasing vulnerability to Soviet defences and the reliance on intercontinental ballistic missiles by the USSR and the USA. While other SAC bombers could convert to low-altitude nuclear strike roles to avoid enemy radar and surface-to-air missiles, the B-36 was designed for high-altitude operations.

Attempting to use the low-altitude bombing system or toss-bombing from low altitude would have imposed crippling structural loads on the 'Peacemaker's' huge airframe. However, in their last year of service, the remaining B-36 wings (including the 72nd BW flying over the Caribbean) did practise long target approaches at altitudes of 200-300 ft, followed by a 'pop-up' to higher altitude for the attack. A radar bomb scoring area in Florida was a usual objective, facing opposition from USAF fighters en route. It was an attempt to simulate what B-36 crews increasingly came to regard as a one-way mission.

CHAPTER SEVEN

MANY CREW, MANY TASKS

The large crew of a B-36, ranging from 15 in D-model bomber versions to more than 23 in RB-36s, often had multiple roles. Gunners doubled as engine scanners, third pilots could be flight engineers and there were usually two radio operators, a spare tail gunner and two flight engineers. The latter added the jet engines to their responsibilities, although their controls were located in a panel above the pilots' positions and their jet instrumentation was limited to a set of warning lights. One of a gunner's secondary roles was removing the safety locks from the upper retraction struts of the main landing gear and replacing them after a flight.

The navigator's role was, in many ways, the most crucial. On missions of more than 30 hours, he would have to keep the bomber on track by old-fashioned dead reckoning, working with the radar officer, who would be following imagery of the ground from his AN/APG-24 (or later model) radar. The two men sat in the same area, assisted by an observer who would take over celestial star-shot duties while the navigator grabbed 30 minutes of sleep periodically on the radio room floor. Frequent sextant star shots were required through the upper observation blister, although visibility was often poor. LORAN (long-range navigation) by radio tower transmissions was available over the US continent, but this was unreliable or usually non-existent over the oceans and beyond.

The navigator's desk was bolted to the left fuselage wall in the radar compartment, which extended into the 'greenhouse' transparency area

B-36H-35 51-5734 of the 26th BS/ 11th BW and star of the *Strategic Air Command* film runs up its engines at Carswell AFB while B-36H-25 51-5721 of the 7th BW takes on fuel. Both wings had relinquished their B-36s by May 1958 (*USAF*)

The radar-bombardier's position, with the search radar scope centrally mounted and the bombsight and Y-3 periscope at the bottom left. The adjacent radio operator also had responsibility for the aircraft's low frequency ECM protection. He had to analyse and record all azimuth data for radar emissions that reached this B-36J (*Author's Collection*)

of the aircraft's nose. In B-36 models with twin nose-gun installations, the navigator also performed a back-up role for the observer who operated those weapons remotely. The flightdeck was above them, housing two pilots and a flight engineer (whose main responsibility was fuel management and monitoring all ten engines with a baffling array of instruments). He would also operate engine fire suppression systems if needed, as well as the oxygen, heating and cabin pressure gauges.

Fuel management on the longest missions, such as 32-hour flights to the forward base at Guam, required particular skill in managing the gauges for a 'max cruise' speed, although return journeys to the USA were usually assisted by strong tailwinds.

During a mission, only pilots and flight engineers were allowed on the flightdeck and all communications with that area were by intercom – most often, these comprised steering corrections from the navigator to the pilot. For a nuclear attack mission, there would have been numerous changes of heading in an attempt to confuse enemy defences.

As the aircraft neared its initial point for a turn towards the target, the pilot handed over control to the radar operator. His radar navigation/attack system then held the aircraft on course to the target automatically until bomb release. At that point the aircraft made a steep climbing turn away from the target at full power. In war, that would have been the only way of at least minimising the effects on the aircraft of a nuclear explosion.

Crews never knew the names of their target cities or towns, only the time scheduled for the mission, from which they could work out where in the eastern Soviet Union they would be heading to attack a pre-determined target. Staging for the outward journey could be made through northerly bases like Thule, in Greenland, while the return trip could include a scheduled forced landing in a desert in Iran.

'Radar' or a 'weaponeer' also had to crawl into the bomb-bay from the radio room during a mission in order to arm the nuclear weapon. This complex task required a reduction in cabin pressure before the crewman could enter the 15-ft-long catwalk to work with the instruments attached to the weapon.

The flightdeck crew would have been the last to leave in an emergency, as they were required to try and control the aircraft while remaining personnel escaped. The two pilots (the aircraft commander and second pilot) and the engineer, therefore, wore back-pack parachutes to save time in a last-ditch emergency, while other crew kept their chest-pack parachutes close at hand.

A typical B-36D training mission profile included a climb to 5000 ft, arming the nuclear weapon and cruising at optimum long-range speeds to a point where the pilot climbed to the chosen combat altitude 500 miles from the simulated target. Fifteen minutes from the target, the speed would be increased for a ten-minute bomb run, followed by two minutes of evasive action and an eight-minute high-speed escape run. At 500 miles from the target, the aircraft descended to cruise altitude. This basic profile was also used by later B-36 models.

SELF-DEFENCE

Within the 'Peacemaker's' ten-year service life, rapid technological advances in defence systems made it a viable combat weapon for only around half that time. In the early years, SAC was preoccupied with overcoming the aircraft's teething troubles and introducing frequent modifications. Seven years after its introduction with the 7th BW, it was clear that the B-36 was no longer able to defeat the rapidly advancing levels of enemy defences. Only delays in the introduction of the B-52 kept the B-36 in limited service as a nuclear bomber until early 1959. In a very different 21st-century strategic situation involving long-range stand-off air-to-ground missiles, it is likely on current estimates that the B-52's service life will be at least ten times as long as the B-36's.

As well as improving their fighter defences, the Soviet Union produced both similar and superior bombers to the B-36. By 1956, the swept-wing, propeller-driven Tu-95 'Bear-D' was entering service. Although it had none of the crew comforts of the B-36, it boasted a 950-mile range, a payload of 65,575 lbs, including the RDS-37 thermonuclear device, and a maximum speed of more than 550 mph. It also rivalled the B-36 as the world's loudest aircraft. Two years earlier, the Tu-16A 'Badger', with twin turbojets, swept wings and nuclear weapons, emerged as a rival to the B-47. With a 7200-mile range and a top speed of 650 mph, it, together with the Tu-95, increased pressure on SAC to produce more B-52s.

As the B-36's *raison d'être* was high-altitude nuclear attacks on communist mainland targets, it was vital to test the aircraft's ability to deploy to suitable foreign airfields and to evaluate its survivability against a variety of interception threats. In the USA, pilots of low-powered early jet fighters like the F-80 were often surprised to find that a B-36, with its much lower wing loading, could out-manoeuvre their nimble fighters at very high altitude or damage them with its slipstream if they closed in from the rear – the most likely direction for an attempted attack.

A hand reaches out from within the B-36 for 20 mm ammunition belts for the tail guns. Each gun's ammunition box held 600 rounds. The turret elevated by 37.5 degrees, aimed down by 36.5 degrees and moved from side to side by up to 45 degrees. Ammunition links and cases were ejected through a chute beneath the turret (*NARA*)

B-36D-50 44-92033 (a 'B-to-D' conversion aircraft), flies in close formation with F-94B Starfire 51-5450 of the Oregon ANG's 142nd Fighter Group during a simulated interception. At high altitude a B-36 could turn to avoid the free-flight rocket armament of the USAF's premier F-89 Scorpion and F-94B interceptors (*Terry Panopalis Collection*)

At 40,000 ft, the margin between maximum speed and stalling speed for a jet was slim, and any manoeuvres beyond a very shallow turn would rapidly precipitate a stall. A B-36 crew approaching a target from unpredictable directions in areas where ground radar and communications networks were patchy stood a good chance of reaching their target before an interception could be organised, even if the fighter pilots could see the bomber or its contrails. Defenders also had to allow for the time taken by a fighter to reach the B-36's altitude and establish an attacking position. In 1949, these revelations reassured proponents of additional B-36 purchases, but they also accelerated the design of more capable interceptors and gave SAC the priority task of destroying the Soviet Long Range Air Force on the ground.

Gunnery training was assisted in October 1949 by the modification of B-36B 44-92042, which had a 35 mm camera fitted in place of one of its tail guns to photograph interceptions by F-80s at various altitudes. A 7th BW B-36B flew practice interceptions with 27th Fighter-Escort Group F-82E Twin Mustang nightfighters. None of these encounters took place above 25,000 ft – well below the bombers' combat ceiling.

One such event resulted in a disastrous collision on 27 April 1951 between an F-51D Mustang and 7th BW B-36D 49-2658 after it had returned to the USA from a deployment to Lakenheath. Four Mustangs from the Oklahoma Air National Guard's 185th Tactical Reconnaissance Squadron were practising diving interceptions on the B-36, passing very close to it. The pilot of the third fighter misjudged his attack and his wingtip cut into the bomber's cockpit.

The four crew in the rear compartment heard a heavy impact as the nose section broke off. Engine noise faded away and the intercom died. They quickly jettisoned their hatches and prepared to bail out, but the remaining airframe suddenly disintegrated, flinging them into space. Both aircraft crashed near Edmond, Oklahoma. Descending beneath their parachutes, surrounded by heavy, jagged debris also on the way down, four crew from the rear compartment landed near Perkins, Oklahoma. MSgt James Wells, whose parachute shroud lines had been struck by a descending turret door, survived an encounter with two guard dogs and arranged for a colleague with a broken leg to be driven to hospital.

Those four rear crew members were the only survivors. Twelve B-36 crewmen and the fighter pilot were killed. Two of the victims, pilot Capt Harold Barry and Lt Ernest Cox, had been among the survivors of the February 1950 'Broken Arrow' crash of B-36B 44-92075. SSgt Dick Thrasher was also a rescued crewman from that disaster over Canada, and he managed to jump from the B-36B as it fell apart after being hit by the Mustang. Like all SAC mishaps, this one was immediately classified as secret and details were not even available to the crew's squadronmates.

BACK TO BOMBS

By June 1954 SAC had four strategic reconnaissance wings flying RB-36s – the 5th SRW at Travis AFB, the 28th SRW at Ellsworth AFB, the 72nd SRW at Ramey AFB and the 99th SRW at Fairchild AFB. The 72nd SRW's B-36D/Es were notorious for oil leaks, and the wing's efficiency was impacted. A more rigid regime under the command of Gen Bertram Harrison from 1955 improved its SAC availability ratings. The wing participated in several deployments to other bases, including a combined visit to its 'war plan recovery bases' in Turkey by 30 of its RB-36D/Es, together with other 'Peacemakers' from Carswell AFB.

Each B-36 squadron initially had a Unit Establishment number of 18 aircraft, but by 1951 this had risen to 31 as production rates increased. By the end of 1951 there were 163 B-36s on strength, including 65 RB-36s. SAC decided at that time to use its RB-47 units as its primary reconnaissance force, so the RB-36 wings were redesignated as strategic bombardment wings, with a secondary reconnaissance role.

However, to revert to the primary nuclear deterrent role from 1 October 1955 all RB-36s had to go through another modification process at Convair as their reconnaissance configuration prevented carriage of large bombs. Several fuselage bulkheads had to be moved or added to provide load-carrying structures for bomb racks, with the UBS weapons carriage system installed in their No 4 bays. The ECM gear in Bay No 4 was moved back into the aft fuselage, and its three 'ferret' radomes were also moved aft. The bomb-bay doors were suitably modified and Norden M-9 bombsights (used in the B-36B) were installed.

All the reconnaissance equipment in the forward bay was retained, and an additional meteorological data-gathering facility was added. Limited weather reconnaissance was possible using instruments in the nose transparency to measure humidity and temperature, and an MA-1 'dropsonde' radiosonde dispenser was fitted in place of the usual strike camera in the rear fuselage cabin to collect further atmospheric data and transmit it.

Constant weight increases due to SAC's insistence on adding ever-more sophisticated equipment, combined with the need to increase the bomber's range and altitude, necessitated a series of Project Featherweight initiatives from January 1954. Weight reduction was seen as a way of removing the need for some of the staging bases en route to targets and the best option for improving maximum altitude performance. For all the B-36 wings, apart from the 42nd BW based in the northeastern state of Maine, it was necessary to operate from a pre-strike staging base, probably outside the USA, in order to fulfil their range objectives with a maximum fuel load.

A reduction in defensive armament and the discarding of removable equipment could see up to 15,000 lbs shed by the B-36, so Featherweight plans focused on reducing the number of gun turrets and ECM installations. The first Featherweight configuration involved removal of all gun turrets, crew catering and rest facilities and conventional bomb racks, but this was considered too drastic. Featherweight II aircraft (indicated by a 'II' suffix after their designation) kept all the above items, but the turrets were modified to allow rapid removal and drag-reducing flush covers were supplied – but seldom fitted – to replace the observation blisters. This programme saved 4800 lbs.

Featherweight III exacted more severe reductions, deleting all the defensive armament apart from the tail turret and its radar. Most of the gunners, including the third pilot/gunner, were no longer required, although some could retain their secondary duties, reducing the crew to 13.

On the bomber's extended flights, the 'crew comforts' in the rear pressurised compartment had offered a little respite from the fatigue, noise and vibration. For Featherweight III, the crew bunks, well-equipped galley, sound proofing and even the carpet and seat armrests had to go. As a result, the rear compartment was noisier than the forward fuselage. Armour panels around the integral fuel tanks in the wing were also removed, as were anti-icing and fuel tank purging systems.

The overall gains in range could approach 40 per cent, and maximum altitude increased to 47,000 or even 50,000 ft. Featherweight III was partly a response to tests with a captured North Korean MiG-15 which showed that a B-36 at its maximum altitude still stood a chance of out-manoeuvring the enemy fighter, despite the MiG's known excellence as a high-altitude interceptor. If the B-36 pilot made his tightest possible turn a MiG-15 was likely to stall and fall away.

Featherweight modifications were applied to all surviving B/RB-36s from the D-model onwards, but some were only taken to Featherweight II level as it was thought that defensive armament might occasionally be required. B-36H 50-1086, with *Miss Featherweight* nose art, was stripped of all non-essential equipment to gather radiation samples in the 1954 'Castle' nuclear tests, and it reportedly reached 59,000 ft.

PHASE-OUT

From February 1956 B-52s had started to reach SAC heavy bomber wings, and early-build B-36s were duly sent to the 3040th Aircraft Storage Depot at Davis-Monthan AFB for reclamation. The deactivation brought an end to B-36 activity at Carswell, with the redistribution of the 7th BW's aircraft to other units and the transfer of the 11th BW to Altus AFB, Oklahoma. After ten years of SAC service from Carswell, the last B-36 left the base on 30 May 1958. An Open House marked the event, during which the final 'Peacemaker' flew in formation with a B-52 and a B-58A Hustler – its successor on the Convair production line.

The fleet was rapidly depleted until only the 95th BW at Biggs AFB and the 72nd BW at Ramey AFB were left. One of the final duties for Biggs-based aircraft was to transport the last of the base's hydrogen bombs to Albuquerque, New Mexico, for decommissioning. Ramey closed down B-36 operations in January 1959 and Biggs followed in February, with the 95th BW flying the final mission on 12 February when B-36J 52-2827 (the last B-36 to be built) flew to Fort Worth for public display. It arrived at a base already filled with 7th BW B-52s, and the 95th BW had soon converted to B-model Stratofortresses and KC-135A tankers.

CHAPTER EIGHT

MASSIVE CHANGES

The B-36's extensive array of defensive guns was steadily reduced during its service life, both to save weight and in recognition of the increasing capability of enemy interceptors and surface to air missiles. However, the potential enemy threats remained, and alternative means of self-defence were explored. As B-36s ranged well beyond the reach of any escorting fighters, several projects were initiated to allow the bombers to carry their own defending aircraft or tactical reconnaissance fighters as passengers. B-29s and B-50s with modified bomb-bays had been used since 1947 to carry experimental 'X-planes' like the X-1 and D-558-II to a high altitude from which they could be launched on brief, rocket-propelled dashes.

Reviving an idea from the 1930s in which the US Navy's airships *Akron* and *Macon* each carried five F9C fighters and a small hangar deck, the tiny XP-85 Goblin jet fighter was designed by McDonnell for the proposed self-defence of the B-36. Its wings, spanning 21 ft, folded vertically to fit inside the aircraft's rear bomb-bay. The compact tail unit had six separate surfaces and its fuselage was only 14 ft 10 in long. A 3000-lb-thrust J34 engine and enough fuel for 20 minutes of flight at speeds up to 648 mph gave it some credibility as a fighter. Four 0.50-cal machine guns were also squeezed into the fuselage, and its total weight was no more than 5600 lbs.

As no B-36 was available to prove the concept, B-29B 44-84111 was converted to carry a Goblin. Launched from a trapeze mechanism

YF-84F 49-2430, with its horizontal stabiliser canted downwards to fit the carrier aircraft's bomb-bay, attempts to engage the trapeze launching and recovery apparatus of JRB-36F 49-2707 (*Terry Panopalis Collection*)

extended from the bomber's belly, the XP-85 was supposed to return to the 'mother ship' and latch onto the trapeze with a hook for recovery after its defensive activities. The B-29 or B-36 would retain some of its bomb load, or alternatively one bomber in an attack formation would carry up to five XP-85s to protect all the other aircraft.

In a very brief test programme that included less than 2.5 hrs of flight time, it quickly became clear that 'hooking' the fighter back on board was far too difficult. Furthermore, the Goblin's performance and handling were below requirements for its fighter role. Seven flights were made, and during one the first Goblin was pulled up by turbulence as it attempted to hook up. The canopy and the pilot's oxygen mask were pulled off, and he was lucky to make a crash landing. Although the second example made more successful recoveries to the bomber, the project was cancelled in October 1949.

In 1952, the same 'parasite' principle was proposed for the B-36D, but the much larger and more capable F-84E Thunderjet (SAC operated six wings of F-84E/Fs for strike, bomber and escort duties at the time) was chosen as a fighter, carried semi-externally like an 'X-plane'. RB-36F 49-2707 became a JRB-36F, with a cradle in its belly that extended to catch a hook fitted above the F-84's nose for launch and recovery. The cradle also engaged hardpoints on the fighter's surface so that it could be pulled up into a semi-submerged location within the bomber. Modified bomb-bay doors fitted around the fighter and extra 'plug' doors extended to fill the gap while the aircraft was flying its mission.

Tests from 23 April 1952 were successful, but SAC policy changed due to the increasing risks being faced by large reconnaissance aircraft overflying enemy territory. Recognising Gen LeMay's emphasis on intelligence gathering, it was now thought that a small tactical reconnaissance jet such as the newly available RF-84F Thunderstreak, launched from a B-36 outside heavy defences, would stand a better chance of survival. It could also carry its own tactical nuclear weapon, as well as external fuel tanks.

A special loading pit was constructed at Fairchild AFB for the FICON. Before take-off, the trapeze was slightly lowered so that the fighter's wings cleared the GRB-36D's retracting landing gear. In flight, the trapeze extended 20 ft so that the RF-84F could be started and launched (*Terry Panopalis Collection*)

SAC wanted 30 B-36 carriers and 75 RF-84Fs, but budgetary restrictions limited the numbers to ten and 25, respectively. Conversion of an initial GRB-36D was completed in February 1955, and an RF-84F was modified as a GRF-84K, with its horizontal stabilisers canted downwards by 23 degrees to fit beneath the bomber, six months later. Its vertical stabiliser fitted into a slot inside the fuselage. When it was winched up into position, the GRF-84K's underwing stores were only inches from the ground.

The 71st SRW (formerly a tactical reconnaissance wing until November 1954), activated under the command of Col Charles McKenna III at Larson AFB, Washington, flew three squadrons equipped with a total of 75 RF-84F/K reconnaissance aircraft from December 1955. It supplied jets and crews to work with the 348th SRS/99th SRW's GRB-36D/F FICON project.

In action, the RF-84F was meant to be transported for around 2800 miles at 25,000 ft until within 800-1000 miles of its photo target. Its pilot, who had been a passenger in the B-36, then negotiated a narrow catwalk to enter his cockpit. He was then lowered on the 'trapeze' and flew off, theoretically evading detection on radar and dodging any attempts at interception by any of the 7000 MiG-15s that the Soviet Union had built to combat US bombers, while his six cameras surveyed the target. With his RF-84F boasting a maximum speed of more than 630 mph, the pilot probably had a good chance of survival. The FICON arrangement gave SAC access to virtually any target in the world.

In six practice penetration missions by slower FICON 1 F-84Es opposed by Air Defence Command F-86 Sabre and F-94 Starfire fighters, only two were intercepted. On return to the GRB-36F, facilitated at night by specially installed lighting and an APX-29A IFF 'rendezvous' set with its antenna above the bomber's fuselage, the F-84E pilot extended the fighter's retractable hook and was retrieved by the cradle. His fighter could be refuelled from the 1140-gallon tank of JP-4 jet fuel installed in the No 4 bomb-bay.

One unexpected recovery occurred in December 1955 when an RF-84K with progressive hydraulic failure was unable to return to base but literally 'hooked up' with a GRB-36D that was in the area, avoiding an ejection by the pilot. Normally in training sorties the fighter would separate from its 'mother ship' and fly back to Larson AFB while the unburdened GRB-36 returned to Fairchild.

The 25 RF-84Ks delivered in 1955-56 saw limited service, which probably included some still-classified flights over Soviet territory, but the project was terminated in 1956 after a collision in which the trapeze apparatus was knocked off a GRB-36D. The difficulty experienced by most RF-84K pilots in safely effecting the link-up on return to the 'mothership' resulted in a number of narrowly avoided accidents. The RF-84Ks were then re-allocated to other units and the strategic reconnaissance mission passed to the high-flying U-2.

Project Tom-Tom was an even more radical approach to carrying self-defence fighters for long-range bombers. Based on a World War 2 concept devised by German aircraft designer Dr Richard Vogt which initially proposed attaching 'free-floating', disposable fuel-containing panels to the outer sections of a bomber's wings, supported by their own lift, it evolved into a plan to connect an escort fighter to each wingtip. German experiments took place in 1945, and in 1949 successful trials were conducted with a C-47A and a PQ-14B Cadet trainer/target drone attached to its wingtip. High-scoring Mustang ace Capt Clarence 'Bud' Anderson, later to command the F-105 Thunderchief-equipped 355th TFW in Vietnam, flew the little PQ-14B.

The idea developed into Project Tip Tow, where two EF-84Ds were attached to an EB-29A by flexible wingtip mounts. Fifteen hours of successful, but risky, flight tests were conducted. During trials of an autopilot to assist the coupling process, an EF-84D flipped over and smashed the wing off the EB-29A. The fighter pilot and four EB-29A crew were killed in the crash, and the project was cancelled.

Tom-Tom sought to apply the same idea to the B-36, with two RF-84Fs attached to JRB-36F 49-2707 through revised linkages. Fifty flight tests with a single RF-84F took place between April and September 1956, with B A Erickson flying either aircraft type. Although the mechanical aspects were sound, the system was very prone to the strong wingtip wake generated by the B-36, and this also caused acute fighter pilot discomfort. On a 26 September flight the latching mechanism engaged asymmetrically, leaving the RF-84F at an unfavourable yaw angle that made the fighter oscillate wildly until it broke off part of the bomber's wingtip. Both aircraft survived, but the project gave way to FICON as a way of extending the RF-84F's range.

Other projected uses of the B-36's prodigious lifting power were drafted, ranging from being a launch platform for the GAM-63 RASCAL or SM-64 Navaho cruise missiles, to 'mothership' for the X-15 high-speed research aircraft, a task later reassigned to the NB-52A. YDB-26H 51-5710 did fly with a 32-ft-long inertially guided GAM-63 under its belly in 1954, and 12 modification kits for operational DB-36H use were produced, but the project was cancelled in July 1955.

TANBO XIV

Using B-36s as aerial tankers was an idea that originated in 1946 when Gen George Kenney was looking for reasons to cancel the B-36 bomber version. It was briefly revived in 1951 as the TANBO (Tanker-Bomber) project, using the British Mk XIV hose, reel and boom system. B-36H 51-5706 was converted in May 1952 to carry the equipment in its No 4 bomb-bay, although it could be removed to allow the bay to be used for ordnance. The other bomb-bays were permanently adapted as jet fuel tanks. The system proved to be too difficult to use, partly due to the lack of suitable fuel hoses, and tests ended in May 1953. By that time the KC-135A tanker was imminent, so TANBO became redundant.

XC-99

As far back as 1942, the prospects of the XB-36 receiving more than a token production contract were greatly enhanced by the USAAF's request for a parallel transport variant in December 1942. By the end of that year, Convair had received a $4.6m contract to work on the Model 37 (XC-99) intercontinental cargo aircraft, with a gigantic fuselage 20.5 ft tall offering 16,000 cubic feet of cargo space mated with the wings, engines and tail unit of the YB-36, including the single-wheel undercarriage of the early bomber version. Multi-wheel bogies were later retrofitted to the prototype.

By 1945, the Model 37 was also being promoted as a luxury 204 passenger 'Super Clipper' airliner. Pan American World Airways pre-ordered 25 for post-war delivery, but the original contract for the XC-99 was a 1942 USAAF order for a prototype, 43-52436.

It could transport 400 troops and eight crew in less luxurious conditions on canvas benches, or 10,000 lbs of cargo over a 10,000-mile range at 292 mph. Alternatives were a 100,000 lbs payload over 1720 miles or 300 casualties on stretchers. Cargo was loaded through two sliding doors and two pairs of clamshell doors under the fuselage, and there were two ramps for vehicles to drive up. There were two decks, the upper deck being a single very long compartment with hoists to load cargo and ladders for crew entry. A rest area behind the cockpit had bunks for long flights, but it lacked the in-built galley of the B-36.

Pan American's interest in the aircraft extended to exploration of a flying boat version of the XC-99 with tractor propellers at a time when the 1930s tradition of long-range commercial seaplane transport was still thought to be viable. In Britain, Saunders-Roe was building its SR.45 Princess, a ten-engined flying boat with a 219 ft-wingspan and 345,000-lb maximum weight.

In November 1947, Howard Hughes' H-4 Hercules ('Spruce Goose') made its only, very brief flight, having consumed $283m in development costs. With an unsurpassed 320-ft wingspan and eight R-4360 engines, it was meant to carry up to 750 troops across the Atlantic, rather than risking them in seaborne convoys. All these projects quickly gave way to land-based transports, although the Princess was considered by the US Navy for a nuclear-powered aircraft project in 1958.

The only XC-99 was passed to the USAF on 26 May 1949, and the San Antonio Air Materiel Area soon put its enormous cargo capacity to good use carrying B-36 components from its base at Kelly AFB to the Convair plant in San Diego. In the aptly named Operation *Elephant*, it took off at weights exceeding 135 tons loaded with R-4360 engines, propellers and other parts, completing a flight at that weight with only five engines operating.

Inspection of the airframe in 1957 showed that structural fatigue was affecting the wings and fuselage bulkheads. Repairs were not considered to be cost effective, and the aircraft was grounded, displayed and eventually donated to the US Air Force Museum in 1993 in severe need of restoration.

The sole XC-99 (43-52436) in service with the San Antonio Air Materiel Area at Kelly AFB with uprated R-4360-41 engines and weather radar, added to the nose in June 1953. Despite failing to engender USAF or commercial production, it led a useful life as a heavy hauler until 1957 (*Terry Panopalis Collection*)

Although Convair redesigned the XC-99 as a production model with a raised B-36B flightdeck and a pressurised upper deck for troop carrying, the USAF saw no need for a C-99, opting instead for more C-97, C-124 and C-133 transports, despite their much smaller interior space. Ironically, sections of the XC-99 were transported to the US Air Force Museum inside a C-5A Galaxy, underlining another change in the USAF's heavy lift policy.

AERIAL REACTOR

The 1940s brought the prospect of nuclear power for both civilian and military purposes, and it was perhaps inevitable that its potential use for the propulsion of ships and submarines would extend to exploration of aircraft applications. In theory, atomic energy offered the prospect of virtually unlimited range and endurance, together with freedom from reliance on conventional fuel supplies. Accordingly, in 1946, the USAAF established the Nuclear Energy for the Propulsion of Aircraft (NEPA) project, and its most obvious primary aim was to explore the installation of a reactor as a power generator for a strategic bomber. NEPA had become the Aircraft Nuclear Program (ANP) by May 1951, which had the support of the Joint Chiefs of Staff.

The first task was to find a suitable proof of concept airborne platform for the heavy reactor, and the B-36 was the obvious choice. In Project MX-1589, NB-36H 51-5712, damaged in the 'Texas Tornado' and then rebuilt, would become the Nuclear Test Aircraft (NTA) – it would be used to explore the requirements for radiation shielding. Two more B-36s, known as X-6s, were to employ a small reactor as a power source. Convair set up a Nuclear Aircraft Research Facility at Fort Worth and contracts were signed in November 1951.

Ground tests of the water-cooled, enriched uranium Aircraft Shield Test Reactor (ASTR) were held, and in 1953 the NB-36H was given a redesigned nose and crew compartment for two pilots, two nuclear engineers and a flight engineer. The entire compartment formed a lead-covered capsule that could be pulled out of the aircraft by a crane for maintenance and decontamination. Flight control cables were attached to rods that could be disconnected easily. Further crew protection was provided by a four-ton lead shielding disc in the second bomb-bay.

The 35,000-lb ASTR was installed in bomb-bay No 4 surrounded by shielding. Water jackets to absorb radiation were located in the fuselage, with several to protect the rear of the crew compartment. Cooling air for the reactor was gathered by large external intakes on

A revised nose section and large external cooling air intakes in place of the lower sighting blisters distinguished the NB-36H (51-5712) from its origins as a B-36H-20. It was a very different aircraft internally, however (*Terry Panopalis Collection*)

the rear fuselage, together with hot air exhausts. The radiation shielding was ground-tested in XB-36 42-13570 that was stored at Fort Worth.

The NB-36H had its nose gear moved forward six inches to allow for a re-sited crew entry hatch. A new windscreen had tinted glass six inches thick. The bomber was stripped of its offensive military equipment and crew facilities. In the new crew compartment the instrumentation was simplified and engine scanning was done through a television system.

The aircraft made the first of 47 test flights on 17 September 1955, with 'Doc' Witchell at the controls. It was accompanied by an instrumented B-50D and a C-97 transport containing armed Marines who would have parachuted in to secure the area if the NB-36H crashed and scattered fission material.

The programme was completed in 1957 and the aircraft was decommissioned and scrapped in September 1958. Doubts about the practicality of attempting to equip and fly the two X-6 aircraft increased after an evaluation in 1953 by President Eisenhower's defense secretary, and they were removed from the 1954 budget. By the end of the NTA evaluation there was little support for any aspect of the programme, and ANP was finally cancelled in March 1961 by President John F Kennedy.

SWEPT-WING 'PEACEMAKER'

In 1951 Convair and Douglas were aware that the USAF was favouring the B-52 as replacement for the B-36, and also that there was no official competition for that contract. Both companies sought ways of presenting alternatives in the hope of changing the USAF's views. Douglas conceived a very large turboprop-powered bomber weighing more than 320,000 lbs and with a range of 11,000 miles.

Convair drafted a six-turboprop design too, but it also pursued jet propulsion ideas, including one with 12 J47s in six underwing pods. The main feature of Convair's initiative was swept flying surfaces linked to a B-36 fuselage (with a nine-foot extension), launched as the B-36G but soon redesignated YB-60 in view of its major differences from other B-36s. The USAF showed tentative interest, ordering prototypes on 15 March 1951 as the XB-60. This involved converting two B-36Fs (49-2676 and 49-2684) from the production line, with an option for production aircraft from March 1953.

As something of a minimum risk venture, using up to three-quarters of the B-36's parts, Convair achieved the swept-back wing changes by using the inner and outer sections of the B-36 wing with a triangular insert to angle the outboard section back by 35 degrees. Another section was added to the leading edge of the inboard wing so that it had a continuous sweep-back from root to tip. Although the wingspan was effectively reduced by 24 ft, the wing area was 500 sq ft greater. New flaps and ailerons were needed. A similar approach was taken to the tail surfaces. The existing B-36 structure was retained but rebuilt at a swept-back angle, with new elevators and rudder.

The engine complement was reduced from 12 J47s to eight Pratt & Whitney J57s in paired underwing nacelles, like the B-52. It retained

The single YB-60 (49-2676) featured roughly 75 per cent B-36F in its structure. Although the aircraft had a larger bomb-bay capacity and longer range than the B-52, its higher, B-36-inherited drag made it more than 100 mph slower with a similar combination of engines to the B-52 (*Terry Panopalis Collection*)

only the tail gun position, rather than the multiple gun turrets of the B-36, which reduced the crew to five in separate compartments without the pressurised communicating tunnel. The smaller B-52 also had a 35-degree sweep, but it benefited greatly from being designed from the outset as a fast jet bomber, albeit with straight wings in the first design proposals.

Production B-60s would have had a crew of nine, adding an engineer/gunner, a tail gunner and two more gunners in the rear compartment, all with sighting blisters and optical gunsights like the B-36. Their two gun turrets would have retracted to conform with the fuselage surface, as would two similar turrets in the upper forward fuselage that were to be manned by the engineer/gunner and navigator gunner in extremis with the aid of an AN/APG-41 radar. A similar radar was provided for the tail gunner, and the search radar beneath the nose was an AN/APS-23. As in-flight refuelling had by then become accepted, Convair included a probe-and-drogue installation for production B-60s.

Manufacture of the two XB-60s proceeded rapidly in 1951, although delays in the supply of J57s prevented completion until April 1952. B A Erickson and 'Doc' Witchell made the first flight on 18 April, three days after Alvin M 'Tex' Johnston had taken the YB-52 aloft on its maiden flight. Informal comparisons soon showed that the B-52 was more than 100 mph faster, and free of the stability problems and control surface buffeting that were apparent in early XB-60 flights.

The USAF only wanted one heavy bomber, and the B-52 was clearly more suitable than the B-60, despite being more costly. After only 66 hours of flight tests, the first XB-60 was grounded, the almost complete second example was earmarked for scrapping and the programme ended. Both were salvaged by July 1954. Commercial applications of the design were considered, but Boeing, once again, clearly had a winner – this time with its Model 707 airliner.

APPENDICES

B-36 UNITS AND BASES

Wing and Squadrons	Base	Tail Marking	Dates
5th BW(H)			
23rd, 31st and 72nd BSs	Fairfield-Suisun/Travis AFB, California	Circle X	14/11/50 to 1/6/58 (originally established as the 5th SRW)
6th BW(H)			
24th, 39th and 40th BSs	Walker AFB, New Mexico	Triangle R	16/6/52 to 1/6/57
7th BW(H)			
9th, 436th and 492nd BSs	Carswell AFB, Texas	Triangle J	1/8/48 to 1/2/58
9th SRW			
1st, 5th and 99th SRSs	Fairfield-Suisun/Travis AFB, California	Circle X	1/5/49 to 1/5/50 (originally established as a Strategic Reconnaissance Wing but redesignated 9th BW(H) on 1 April 1950 and became a B-29 wing in November 1950)
11th BW(H)			
26th, 42nd and 98th BSs	Carswell AFB, Texas	Triangle U	18/11/48 to 1/10/57
28th SRW			
77th, 717th and 718th SRSs	Rapid City/Ellsworth AFB, South Dakota	Triangle S	16/5/49 to 1/2/57 (originally established as the 28th BW(H))
42nd BW(H)			
69th, 70th and 75th BSs	Limestone/Loring AFB, Maine	(none)	25/2/53 to 1/12/55
72nd BW(H)			
60th, 73rd and 301st BSs	Ramey AFB, Puerto Rico	Square F	16/6/52 to 1/1/59 (originally established as the 72nd SRW)
92nd BW(H)			
325th, 326th and 327th BSs	Fairchild AFB, Washington	Circle W	16/6/51 to 15/11/56
95th BW(H)			
334th, 335th and 336th BSs	Biggs AFB, Texas	(none)	8/11/52 to 1/1/59
99th SRW			
346th, 347th and 348th SRSs	Fairchild AFB, Washington	Circle I	1/1/53 to 4/9/56

COLOUR PLATES

1
B-36A-5-CF 44-92009, Carswell AFB, Texas, early 1948
'BM' buzz number codes were assigned to the B-36 from September 1947 through to 1949, although the requirement for heavy bombers to display them was deleted in March 1948. On some early aircraft, the buzz number also appeared under the left wing. BM-009 was the eighth B-36 airframe built, and it was delivered to the Eighth Air Force in June 1948 and later converted, like most B-36As, into RB-36E-5-CF configuration with subsequent Featherweight III modifications. The 21 B-36As carried no defensive armament.

2
B-36A-10-CF 44-92013 of the 7th BW(H), Carswell AFB, Texas, 1948
Delivered to the 7th BW in July 1948, this aircraft was re-manufactured as an RB-36E and finally salvaged in 1957. It flew the third simulated tactical mission on 18-19 July 1948 (a 5983-mile marathon), dropping 31 dummy 500-lb bombs to demonstrate the bomber's capability to a sceptical Congress. For that demonstration, it averaged 301 mph, taking 1 hr 23 min to climb to 26,000 ft with 144,819 lbs of fuel on board when it took off.

3
B-36B-5-CF 44-92038 of the 7th BW(H), Carswell AFB, 1949
The Cold War required SAC's bombers to operate over the Arctic region to maximise their range against potential targets. The Project GEM factory-applied red paint scheme seen on 44-92038 made the aircraft visible if it was forced down on Arctic terrain. The tail was likely to still be intact even if the rest of the aircraft was badly damaged, hence its repainting. Some examples only had red paint on the undersides of the forward part of the horizontal stabiliser. This example later became a B-36D-10-CF, but it was written off with the 7th BW following a ground fire during refuelling at Convair's San Diego facility on 12 June 1952.

4
B-36B-15-CF 44-92073 of the 7th BW(H), Carswell AFB, Texas, May 1950
Delivered to the 7th BW in July 1949, this example was converted

into a B-36D-40-CF as part of the 'B to D' programme, remaining in service, with Featherweight III modifications, until 1957. By September 1952 the B-36s of the 7th and 11th BW(H)s at Carswell AFB comprised two-thirds of SAC's intercontinental bomber force. Geometric tail-codes were inherited from Eighth Air Force use in the late 1940s on B-29s. Nine SAC B-36 wings carried their own versions between 1948 and 1953, using triangles, circles (Fifteenth Air Force) or squares (Second Air Force) depending on their assignment. Buzz numbers had gone by May 1950.

5
B-36D-1-CF 44-92097 of the 7th BW(H), Carswell AFB, 1951

An abbreviated '097' version of the buzz number (later re-painted as '2097') was used by 1951, along with the small *UNITED STATES AIR FORCE* titling, on the forward fuselage. This aircraft, delivered to Carswell in July 1950, was damaged there on 1 September 1952 in the 'Texas tornado' devastation. '097' was blown against B-36H 50-1096, tearing into its right wing and tail area. Repairs to this aircraft alone cost more than $1m. It was written off on 28 August 1954 at Biggs AFB following a miscalculated landing approach after suffering in-flight fuel starvation.

6
B-36D-25-CF 49-2658 of the 26th BS(H)/7th BW(H), Carswell AFB, Texas, 1951

This B-36D was delivered in August 1950, and it visited Lakenheath in January 1951 along with five other B-36Ds for Operation *UK* – the first such deployment by 'Peacemakers'. Like the wing's previous B-29s, the bombers took part in simulated attacks on targets in Europe and interception practice with RAF fighters. Upon its return to Texas, the aircraft was lost following a mid-air collision with an F-51D over Oklahoma on 27 April 1951. Only four crew in the aft compartment were able to escape before the bomber crashed.

7
B-36B-1-CF 44-92037 of the 42nd BW(H), Loring AFB, Maine, 1955

Delivered in December 1948, '037' (depicted here with its forward upper turret deployed) became a B-36D-40-CF 'B-to-D' conversion and received Featherweight II updates. The 42nd BW began B-36 operations in April 1953 at Loring AFB, which had been built specifically for the 'Peacemaker'. The largest SAC base in the USA, it was among only three with a hangar large enough to house two B-36s. This aircraft is finished in silver lacquer overall, with typically restrained SAC markings. The 36-inch *U.S. AIR FORCE* marking became standard in 1955, generally displacing buzz numbers.

8
B-36D-45-CF (rebuilt B-36B-15-CF) 44-92065 of the 326th BS(H)/92nd BW(H), Fairchild AFB, Washington, May 1955

The 92nd BW at Fairchild AFB exchanged its B-29s for B-36s from 20 July 1951 and began large-scale deployments to the Far East and Guam in 1953. By 1957 it had converted to B-52s. The wing used prehistoric characters devised by V T Hamlin for the 'Alley Oop' cartoon strip as unit insignia. 'Alley Oop' rode his brontosaurus 'Dinny' in the image used by the 326th BS on the noses of its silver-lacquered B-36Ds.

9
RB-36D-15-CF 49-2695 of the 5th SRW, Travis AFB, California, August 1952

Delivered as an RB-36D in December 1950, this aircraft was later converted into one of ten GRB-36D-15-CFs for use in the FICON project. The rework included Featherweight III modifications. With the 5th SRW, it operated from Travis AFB, which had B-36s for almost eight years. Once converted into GRB-36D, the aircraft joined the 99th SRW for FICON use. Sent to the Arizona Aircraft Storage Squadron at Davis-Monthan in 1956, it was scrapped there by Mar-Pak the following year.

10
RB-36E-10-CF (rebuilt B-36A-15-CF) 44-92023 of the 72nd BS(H)/5th BW(H), Travis AFB, California, August 1952

This aircraft was one of the initial batch of 22 B-36As (and the YB-36) from 1948 that were disassembled and rebuilt as RB-36Es in 1950-51, the bombers being fitted with jet pods, 20 mm armament and ECM and reconnaissance equipment in a remanufactured fuselage. It also received Featherweight II updates, and remained in use until 1957. The 'Circle X' marking on the tail indicated that the 5th BW was assigned to the Fifteenth Air Force.

11
GRB-36D-1-CF 44-92092 of the 348th SRS/99th SRW, Fairchild AFB, Washington, 1955

Modified bomb-doors to fit around its passenger RF-84F and an APX-29A beacon above the fuselage distinguish this FICON aircraft from the standard RB-36D externally. There were also considerable internal changes made to allow the aircraft to accommodate the parasite fighter, its trapeze system and fuel supply. The RF-84F came from the 91st SRS/71st SRW at Larson AFB. The GRB-36D, originally a B-36B, displays another combination of a partial buzz number with the *U.S. AIR FORCE* titling.

12
B-36D-50-CF 44-92033 (rebuilt B-36B-1) of the 92nd BW(H), Fairchild AFB, Washington, 1956

A 1955 revision to the B-36 bomber force added 200 lbs of reflective white paint to large areas of the aircrafts' undersurfaces, with clear or silver acrylic lacquer on the uppersurfaces. It provided some protection from nuclear radiation. The *USAF* titling beneath the left wing was usually removed when the white finish was applied. The SAC shield and banner were also displayed on most B-36s by this time, with unit insignia generally replacing the shield on the starboard side. As a B-36B-1-CF, this aircraft had the red Arctic scheme before its 'B to D' conversion and Featherweight II updates.

13
RB-36D-10-CF 49-2688 of the 28th BW(H), Ellsworth AFB, South Dakota, 1954

The 28th BW was one of the earliest B-36 operators, flying the bomber between July 1949 and May 1957. This example was delivered in September 1950 when the base was known as Rapid City AFB. A solitary arch hangar provided some protection for groundcrew from the hard winter weather when undertaking maintenance on a single B-36. 49-2688 received Featherweight II modifications and was eventually scrapped in 1957.

14
B-36F-5-CF 49-2680 of the 39th BS(H)/6th BW(H), Walker AFB, New Mexico, May 1956

On this Featherweight II aircraft, the 'last three' of the serial appear in a smaller style ahead of the *U.S. AIR FORCE* titling and behind the squadron's 'pirate' insignia, which originated in 1919 when the wing's predecessor operated in the Panama Canal Zone as the 3rd Observation Group. 49-2680 retained its gun turrets and sighting blisters as part of Featherweight II. The bomber flew from September 1951 until it was scrapped in 1957.

15
RB-36F-1-CF 49-2704 of the 31st SRS/5th SRW, Travis AFB, California, 1954

A Fifteenth Air Force aircraft, 49-2704 was delivered in July 1951 following its first flight on 30 April as part of a batch of only 24 RB-36Fs manufactured up to December of that year. These aircraft used similar reconnaissance equipment to the RB-36D, together with the more powerful water-alcohol-injected R-4360-54 engines of the B-36F. One RB-36F (49-2707) was used as the test aircraft for the Tom-Tom and FICON projects. By mid-1958 only 19 RB-36Fs remained in use.

16
RB-36F-1-CF 49-2703 of the 348th SRS/99th SRW, Fairchild AFB, Washington, July 1955

This aircraft's crew achieved fame for demonstrating SAC's 'press on' policy on 11 July 1955. Appearing with eight other B-36s in a flypast for the inauguration of the Air Force Academy, the bomber lost its rudder near Denver, Colorado. Pilot Maj William Deyerle used his throttles and ailerons to maintain control and landed safely at Ellsworth AFB – a feat that earned him the Distinguished Flying Cross for saving a $4.1m bomber and its crew. The 99th SRW had been activated at Fairchild AFB on 1 January 1953 under Col Salvatore E Manzo with RB-36s and RB-29s.

17
B-36H-5-CF 50-1092 of the 11th BW(H), Carswell AFB, Texas, 1952

This aircraft features the 11th BW's 'Grey Geese' insignia on its nose, this marking originating when the wing flew B-17s and B-24s in the Far East during World War 2. The 11th BW shared the service introduction of the B-36 with the 7th BW, and it re-equipped several times with new variants of the 'Peacemaker'. The wing provided aircraft for the Hollywood motion picture *Strategic Air Command* and made the B-36's first deployment to North Africa in December 1951. The 11th BW participated in the December 1951 RAF Bombing Competition, although the prizes went to B-29 squadrons.

18
RB-36F-1-CF 49-2708 of the 99th SRW, Fairchild AFB, Washington, August 1954

Foreign deployments by reconnaissance B-36s included several to Britain, where aircraft participated in a series of Roundout reconnaissance missions that took place over two years until RB-47Es assumed the role in 1954. This example was among the RB-36Fs that undertook the final deployment to Fairford. RB-36s of the 5th and 28th SRWs also rotated through British bases for Roundout.

19
RB-36D-10-CF 49-2691 of the 28th SRW, Ellsworth AFB, South Dakota, 1952

RB-36Ds preceded B-36Ds in SAC service in June 1950, and all 24 'new build' examples went to the 28th SRW from June 1951. In January of that year an RB-36D had made the longest B-36 flight ever recorded, staying aloft for 51.5 hours. The three 'ferret' ECM antennae under the fuselage, in a location corresponding to the No 4 bomb-bay, were moved further aft when the bay was used for nuclear weapons.

20
RB-36E (rebuilt B-36A-10-CF) 44-92014 of the 301st SRS/72nd SRW, Ramey AFB, Puerto Rico, 1954

Named after Maj Gen Roger Ramey, commander of the Eighth Air Force from 1946 to 1950, Ramey AFB at Aguadilla in northwest Puerto Rico had an 11,702 ft x 200 ft runway specifically built for the 72nd SRW's RB-36s to use from 16 June 1952 until January 1959. 44-92014's tail marking indicated the wing's assignment to the Second Air Force, although tail markings were often removed when reconnaissance aircraft deployed to bases close to hostile territory.

21
B-36D-50-CF (rebuilt B-36B-20-CF) 44-92061 of the 325th BS/92nd BW, Fairchild AFB, Washington, 1952

This, the final 'B-to-D' conversion to leave Convair's San Diego facility, was among the 'Peacemakers' to visit Britain in the early 1950s. The wing's pterodactyl squadron emblem (which adorned the noses of its B-36s from June 1952) and 'Higher, Stronger, Faster' motto dated back to its Eighth Air Force days in World War 2, when the 92nd BG flew B-17s as 'Fame's Favoured Few'.

22
B-36H-10-CF 51-5704 of the 7th BW, Carswell AFB, Texas, 1958

Delivered in October 1952, this B-52H had Featherweight III modifications, including the removal of defensive armament (apart from the tail turret) and the upper forward sighting blisters. White 'High Altitude Camouflage' included 20 gallons of gloss white enamel anti-flash paint from February 1955. Its silver uppersurfaces are relieved by the revised 7th BW insignia on the nose atop the SAC banner. The lower aft blisters were retained partly to allow crewmen to make visual engine checks in flight.

23
B-36H-1-CF 50-1086 of the 7th BW, Eglin AFB, Florida, October 1955

Project Featherweight, begun in January 1954, added almost 39 per cent extra range by removing up to 15,000 lbs of weight. Christened *Miss Featherweight*, 50-1086 received Phase II modifications in that programme and retained its observation blisters, but lost the nose turret. Featherweight III reductions came later. This aircraft flew trials with various heavy ordnance at Eglin AFB and participated in Operation *Castle* in 1954, gathering atmospheric radiation samples.

24
JB-36H-55-CF 52-1358 of the 4925th Test Group (Atomic), Kirtland AFB, New Mexico, 1957

This was one of a pair of similarly painted JB-36Hs, previously designated EB-36Hs until 1955, used as high-altitude photographic targets for missile tracking cameras at the Atlantic Missile Range at Cape Canaveral, Florida. Sister ship 52-1357 was also used to support the Operation *Redwing* nuclear test programme in 1956.

25
RB-36H-10-CF 51-5743 of the 4925th Test Group (Atomic), Kirtland AFB, New Mexico, 1955

This aircraft participated in the Operation *Teapot* nuclear weapons trials over the Nevada test site in early 1955. Fourteen drops were made in which B-36s delivered two types of weapons with warheads of up to 3.2 kilotons in *Shot Wasp*, *Wasp High*, *Shot High* and *Wasp Prime* trials. During the *Teapot* tests, the 4925th Test Group, under the auspices of the Armed Forces Special Weapons Project and the Air Force Special Weapons Center, drew on aircraft from all four of SAC's Strategic Reconnaissance Wings. The *Teapot* RB-36s were usually operated with most of their unit markings removed, although 51-5743 has retained the 'Triangle S' of the 28th SRW – the unit that supplied it to the 4925th Test Group.

26
RB-36H-15-CF 51-5748 of the 28th SRW, Ellsworth AFB, South Dakota, 1952

The 28th SRW made its first British deployment, to Fairford, from 2 September to 8 December 1952 (with diversions to Upper Heyford), and it followed this up with two more visits in 1953 for Roundout reconnaissance missions within 200 miles of communist countries. This particular aircraft was also transferred from the 28th SRW to Kirtland AFB for service with the 4925th Test Group as a JRB-36H. The 'Peacemaker' was used as a camera platform for *Hardtack* high-altitude atomic tests undertaken in 1958.

27
B-36H-25-CF 51-5722 of the 11th BW, Carswell AFB, Texas, 1957

This Featherweight III B-36H displays the 11th BW patch on its nose and typically plain exterior. The blanked-off circular panel on the nose transparency indicates installation of a Y-3 periscopic

bombsight in place of the Norden version, which remained in RB-36s. This aircraft was scrapped a year later within a few weeks of its retirement, after only five years' service.

28
RB-36H-20-CF 51-5754 of the 72nd SRW, Ramey AFB, Puerto Rico, 1955

Delivered to SAC in May 1952, this RB-36H displays the 72nd SRW insignia on its nose and anti-flash paintwork. The wing had an exceptional safety record, suffering only one loss (51-5745, the last of 32 B-36s destroyed in USAF service) from an explosion and ground fire in November 1957. This example received Featherweight II updates, and it was among the last 'Peacemakers' to be scrapped in 1959.

29
B-36J-10-CF(III) 52-2824 of the 327th BS/92nd BW, Fairchild AFB, Washington, July 1956

One the last four B-36s to be produced in the final batch of 14 J-models (the only B-36s to be manufactured as Featherweight IIIs), this aircraft was a 'sampler' for the *Redwing* atomic bomb tests of 1956, fitted with an external box behind its cockpit to collect radioactive particles.

30
B-36J-1-CF 52-2220 of the 95th BW, Biggs AFB, El Paso, Texas, 1958

Delivered to SAC in January 1954, this B-36J served with the 95th BW, which, along with the 72nd BW, was the last operational 'Peacemaker' unit. It retained the markings of the 95th in storage at Davis-Monthan. Donated to the USAF Museum at Wright-Patterson AFB, 52-2220 became the last B-36 to fly when the bomber made its delivery flight to the museum at Dayton, Ohio, on 30 April 1959. The aircraft remained in outdoor storage, completing 11 years of exposure to the elements without suffering substantial deterioration. Fully restored, the bomber replaced the museum's YB-36/RB-36E as the centrepiece of the Air Power Gallery in the museum's new main building in 1971.

7th BW B-52H-10 51-5704 leads its successors, a B-52 and a prototype B-58A, in the farewell flypast for the 'Peacemaker' at Carswell on 30 May 1958 (*Terry Panopalis Collection*)

INDEX